Advance Praise

No! Your Other Left Foot is a superb and charming story, as original as its title. If you believe a woman's life ends at sixty, think again. Thea Clark proves that excitement, competitiveness, and a lust for living persist indefinitely in the woman who dares to strip down to her skin, don a flashy costume, and come out ready to dance!

    Maralys Wills, author of *Higher Than Eagles*

Thea Clark's *No! Your Other Left Foot* is a story about daring. In her sixties, she dared to get out of her easy chair, defy her elderly mother, and step into a new world of competitive ballroom dancing. She dared to care about her handsome young dance instructor and to care *for* him when he was struck down with a tragic illness. Although still grieving, she couldn't give up the joy her body experienced in motion to music and fancy footwork and moved on with a new dance instructor. For hours of unique entertainment, give Thea Clark's memoir a whirl—and be inspired to take up a daring adventure of your own.

    Barbara French, author of *Someday Street*

No! Your Other Left Foot

Ballroom Dancing My Way Through My 60s

Thea B. Clark

Forked Road Press

Copyright 2012 © Thea B. Clark

ISBN 978-0-9801165-1-9

All rights reserved. No part of this book may be reproduced or transmitted in any form or by any means, electronic or mechanical, including photocopying and recording by an information recording and retrieval system, without express written permission from the publisher.

Forked Road Press
2373 N. Flower St.
Santa Ana, CA 92706
www.forkedroadpress.com

To contact the author: dancelady29@gmail.com

Some of the personal names in this memoir were changed for the purpose of privacy.

Manufactured in the United States of America

LIBRARY OF CONGRESS CONTROL NUMBER: 2012943339

Cover design: Stephanie Starr
Cover photo: Tim W. McCray
Back cover portrait photo: Tod Kim
Interior dance graphic: Tina Syrengelas

Dedication

THIS BOOK IS DEDICATED to my mother, Althea Edwina Faucett Bryant. Brave, determined, fiercely loyal, unflinchingly committed to the welfare of my father and me, she was never hesitant about meeting a problem head-on. She encouraged me to follow my own artistic yearnings. If by helping me she'd had to leap tall buildings in a single bound, she'd have tried. I miss her Scorpio stingers.

She was rare among the mothers of my friends. She was Martha Stewart at home: painting, plastering, gardening. She was courageous, driving from the Atlantic Seaboard to the Pacific Ocean during the WWII gas-rationing crisis with a six-year-old daughter as navigator. I miss her Down-East common sense grounding me.

She might not have cared much for this book, but she would have been proud of me for writing it. Unexpectedly shy among strangers, she would have hawked my book on street corners if I'd asked. She believed in other worlds, and that we are all forever connected while committed to lifelong learning. She was an old soul and destined not to return but to move on, giving advice wherever she landed.

Thank you, Mom, for being my "old trout."

Sherrie Shepherd of the television talk show *The View* said, when she was booted off *Dancing With the Stars,* "Run toward your fear."
I sat in the studio audience of that very first season in 2005 and knew then that *DWTS* would be a lollapalooza of a show.

Table of Contents

Introduction

1. A Pair of La-Z-Boys • *1*
2. How Did I Land Among These Peacocks • *3*
3. Pesky Man, Fateful Night • *9*
4. Suckerrr!! • *12*
5. The Road to Oz • 18
6. If I Weren't So Old and Straight • *24*
7. Just Use Your Other Left Foot • 27
8. A Secret Life • 33
9. Now, I'm a Ballroom Mom • 38
10. Michael's Health Problems Escalate • 45
11. When Does Two Become One • 50
12. Disaster in Blue • 63
13. Sixty-three Plus and Still My Mother's Child • 68
14. $250 a Minute • *70*
15. What's a Body Suit? • *75*
16. Nana and Luke • *90*
17. Las Vegas • *96*
18. Glitz, Glitter, Glamour • *102*
19. The Dreaded Cha Cha Cha • *110*
20. Nana Disappears • *113*
21. Michael's Teaching Days End • *115*
22. Jealousy Was a Tango • 116
23. Help! I'm Going to Kill Myself • 130
24. A House Is Not a Home When It's A Hospice • *133*
25. Lewis Suarez • 137
26. Jolene's Fifteen Minutes of Fame • *141*
27. A Doppelganger Or? • *143*
28. Bereft • *150*

29. Master Teacher • *152*
30. Another Route to Oz • *156*
31. Dancing in a War Zone • *160*
32. An Oasis of Elegance Amidst a Racial Tsunami • *167*
33. We Close the Competition • *173*
34. I Dance for Fun and Friends • *179*
35. Happy Birthday to Me • *183*
36. Luke Surprises Me • 197
37. A New Studio • 204
38. The Korean Show • 209
39. Surviving the Korean Show • *222*
40. The Cavalry • *225*
41. A Dip to Build a Dream on • *226*
42. The New Me • *229*
43. Arizona for Two • *231*
44. Goodbye to Nana and Michael • *237*
45. Ramon, the Fearsome • *243*
46. Twenty-one Steps • *246*
47. The Pain • *249*
48. To Be in Shock, or Not to Be • *256*
49. Toof? What Toof? • *265*
50. Back to Work Too Soon • *276*
51. Twenty-One Steps Revisited • 278
52. My Next Challenge • *284*
53. Stubbornness, Thy Name is Thea • *286*
54. Lewis Pulls Me Through Again • 294
55. Florida • 296
56. Side Slits • 302
57. Trust Me, He Said • 304
Acknowledgments

Welcome, Friend, to My Story

At age thirty, forty, and most certainly at fifty, I wouldn't have imagined myself stark naked in a dressing room full of Barbie lookalikes. To wear sexy Latin dance costumes, you undress all the way. Neither could I have fantasized that in my sixties I'd be on a darkened stage bathed by a brilliant spotlight, performing a tango with a handsome man forty years my junior. And how then could I have anticipated the sorrow that would rock me when my first teacher died of AIDS?

If work defined me, who was I when I retired?

How could I prepare to go from something to nothing?

No! Your Other Left Foot: Ballroom Dancing My Way Through My 60s is an if-I-can-do-it-so-can-you memoir of my journey from couch potato to passionate dancer. Complicating this trip was an angst-filled grandson and my mother's waning years.

The best things in life are free.

Wrong.

Sometimes they cost thousands.

No! Your Other Left Foot

1

A Pair of La-Z-Boys

"You're getting to be a frumpy, dumpy, little old lady," said the white-haired mound to my left.

I was sixty-one; she was ninety-three.

She leaned across the tray table between us, stabbed her finger at my belly. "You're getting fat. And since you retired, you're really bossy."

If my mother's words had color they'd be acid green.

Apathy, my current mantra, permeated the air like L.A. smog. Even the family room's super-sized orange and red poppy wallpaper, chosen in a moment of whimsy, expressed more energy.

Early October rain rattled the large sliding door behind us, sending swift cascades down the glass and onto the patio bricks. The decades-old song "It Never Rains in Southern California" accompanied images of Malibu mudslides and freeway havoc, flashing like an old-fashioned newsreel on the big blue eye of the TV.

Frumpy, dumpy, indeed. While I'd never considered myself remotely glamorous, my mother's words stung. I slowly counted to ten. In the flickering, eerie light, she missed seeing me stick out my tongue. *One more crack like that and it's the nursing home for you, Old Trout.*

She grunted. "You need a hobby, or a man, or both."

My jaw clenched. Still, I kept silent; she paid half the rent.

The kitchen phone jangled, jarring us both. I didn't move.

"Aren't you going to answer that?"

Sighing, I managed, just barely, to heave my frumpy, dumpy, bossy, hobby-less, man-less rump out of the chair and answer "Hello!"

"Good evening," said an enthusiastic male voice. "Our studio is offering a free dance lesson."

Holy cannoli! How many suckers do they snooker with these so-called free lessons? "Sorry. Not interested." I slammed down the receiver.

"Who's on the phone?" asked my elderly roomie.

"Nobody, Nana."

"Had to be somebody. I saw your mouth move. Or were you eating again?"

I sighed. "A man selling ballroom dance lessons."

"Ha," Mother howled. "You dancing! That would be something for the *Guinness Book of World Records*."

Dance lessons. Me? Why? What a foolish idea. I'd have to be crazy—wouldn't I?

Wouldn't I?

2

How Did I Land Among These Peacocks

A ROLLER COASTER of a year later, I strode into a Las Vegas hotel ballroom, my hand clasped by the cool fingers of a handsome young man in white tie and tails. Head held high, I felt like a matador marching into an arena, the audience exploding with the welcoming screams of aficionados. My suit of lights was a blushing peach satin gown encrusted with Swarovski crystals, flashing and sparkling.

What had transpired following the couch potato scene with my mother and that irritating phone call? What led to this moment? If those in the audience only knew: more than a hundred hours of private lessons, two local competitions, and a near disaster in a Christmas show.

Now, back to that huge Las Vegas ballroom where dozens of competitors waited on the sidelines for their chance to perform.

"Thea," said handsome Michael, "don't be nervous."

I groaned.

He pointed to my knees vibrating my new satin skirt and chuckled, then he patted my shoulder. "You'll be fine. Ready?" Spine straight and elegant in his Fred Astaire attire, Michael's full height seemed electric with anticipation. "Show confidence. Stroll like a queen. Smile at your subjects."

He tucked my arm in his and squeezed my fingers.

Looking over my shoulder at the other C Division women lined up in back of us, I wondered. Are they as jittery as me? I imagined I heard an echo of the opening bars of "Our Hearts Were Young and Gay." Heck, it fit. I was young at heart and, yes—he was gay.

I surveyed this tall, elegant young 'un, then my eyes roved over the audience occupying the bleachers of the Las Vegas Hilton. I couldn't believe they had actually paid to watch us. I sized up my competition, women in the fifty- to sixty-five-year-old category, all glamorous in satins, sequins, and feathers, nails manicured and pedicured, professionally coiffed. Really, how did I, a sixty-plus retired junior high school teacher, land among these birds of paradise?

Michael interrupted my musings. "Pay attention. Tonight, you dance one heat right after the other, a waltz, a foxtrot, and an American tango."

"Yes. You've already told me that."

Using a softer tone and in a slower cadence, "I want you to be clear. The heats move along fast."

"Really? No pause in between to get a drink or sit down?"

"Right."

I stared at him. "Why didn't you explain this before?"

"I didn't want to freak you out. Now, when the announcer calls our names, suck in your stomach and smile."

A no-nonsense business-suited lady with a clipboard diligently kept track of the entrants. Standing at the edge of the dance floor, she tapped Michael on the shoulder. "Off you go and good luck."

Stepping from the carpet onto the polished hardwood, I entered another dimension. With my favorite music genre, the waltz, swirling around me, I counted to myself, one, two, three, one, two, three, over and over. The rhythm of "Moon River" syncopated with my heart and I floated in Michael's arms, oblivious to the current of other dancers moving in line-of-dance around the super-sized parquet floor. *This reminds me of my high school roller skating days with my favorite beau, and the pounding beat of the Wurlitzer pulling us around the rink to The Tennessee Waltz. Heaven!*

"Don't lose focus," Michael whispered in my ear. "Pay attention."

My stomach lurched.

"We'll circle the floor until we've been seen by all eight judges. Keep looking past my right shoulder and up toward the ceiling."

"I know, I know. It's framing."

"Shush. I do the talking." And, he did, without moving his lips, using the entire intense ninety seconds.

Eighteen of us danced counter-clockwise, synchronized like the grand MGM musicals of the nineteen thirties and forties.

"Keep you upper body still," Michael said. "Move from the hips. My body's momentum will move you backwards."

He makes it sound so effortless, I thought, concentrating on his commands, sensing only his body and the electric space between us. *Dear God, thank you. Thank you. I feel wonderful.*

Abruptly, he pulled me to a stop. "Good job." He hustled me off the parquet only to turn me around at the edge of the dance floor with "Be still. Listen to the announcer."

"Six couples will return for a semi-final waltz," said the emcee at the podium. "They are: number forty-five, and…"

"Yes!" said Michael and gestured with his free hand as though pulling down the handle of a slot machine.

When the announcer had recalled all six couples and we'd moved forward away from the pack, the remaining dancers left the floor in disappointment.

I'm sorry for them all, but I'm sure glad it's not me.

Michael touched the tip of my nose. "Don't get overconfident. It's okay to have fun but technique counts."

With a shiver I was back at junior high gym class, among the last to be picked for the next dance. Get over it. Now here I was fifty years later, paying close attention to the commands of a man a third my age. I'd definitely moved beyond my comfort zone. I embraced the vision of a young Dorothy skipping toward Emerald City, dancing on her Yellow Brick Road into the unknown.

Within the next half hour we had scored in the top three. I walked off the floor after the last heat in a daze.

Afterward we joined Patty, an advanced student stunning that night in her bright red-feathered gown. She'd performed after my heats and before the awards for my division. She clapped her hands and said with delight, "Thea, you looked like Cinderella in that dress."

I gave her a hug. "I love this dress. I really do feel like Cinderella. Thank you for telling me about Mr. Suarez. I like his design." Fanning my skirt and fluffing my feathers carefully, I sank into my chair, trembling with relief, my muscles collapsing after the high alert tension. "Are we done for today?"

Michael nodded, his eyes searching the room for friends. "Excuse me, Miss Thea." He offered that lovely grin. "I'll see you tomorrow morning, seven thirty."

Ready to leave, my dance bag packed and zipped, I heard Patty ask, "What are you wearing for the Latin?"

"A simple shift with long sleeves, completely covered with silver sequins."

"Sounds good. See you around eight."

I followed her exit from the ballroom. How lucky to be tall and slim with long graceful legs. Maybe in my next life, I'll look like that.

In the morning, wearing my sparkly dress and silver dance shoes, I made my way through the stale smoke of the all-night gamblers.

Patty met me at the entrance. "I came to root for you," she said, smiling.

I was about to thank her when the emcee called for the Newcomers' rumba. Michael and I were competing against most of the same group of couples from the day before. I did okay; the ruffle wobbled and my hips gyrated. Michael smiled as we hurried to the head of the line once again. "Cha cha next," he said.

During lessons I'd had trouble with the introductory step, often starting on the wrong foot.

Michael placed us in the exact center of the floor where we were visible to all the judges. As he turned me to face him, I froze, rigid as a fence post set in cement.

"Thea! Arms up."

For ninety seconds I was semi-conscious, coming to when Michael tugged me off the floor.

"Don't sit down. Swing comes next," he said.

"No worries," I said breathing hard. *The worst is over.*

A half hour later when the awards were announced, I gasped. I'd been awarded a Third in cha cha. By 9:30 a.m. my first dance competition was over. I'd taken two Firsts, two Seconds, and two Thirds in the Latin division, and I'd done even better in the Smooths.

Hallelujah! Time to put the La-Z-Boy in the garage.

3

Pesky Man, Fateful Night

THAT NIGHT WHEN Harry the telemarketer had first called —was that only a year ago?—after hanging up the phone I remember saying to Nana, "I'm bored with the storm news repeated over and over. It's like we never have weather like this in Southern California. Slowly rising from the cushy comfort of my La-Z-Boy, I sighed. "I'm going upstairs to read."

"Fine," said Old Trout. "I'll go, too."

I clicked off the TV. "Need help getting up?"

"Humpf!" she grunted. "I'm hard of hearing and can barely see, but I can still get in and out of my chair by myself, thank you, Missy."

I followed behind her slow limp through the living room. At the stairs, she clawed the wrought iron banister to pull herself up. I contemplated what would happen if she fell back. Even though she was her thinnest ever, was I in any condition to catch her? I quickly placed my hand on her boney rump.

Again she humpfed. Finally reaching the top, she turned and with our faces almost touching, her eyes flashing, she grinned. "See? Made it again."

Upstairs, thunder shook the windows. The eucalyptus tree outside her bedroom window was floodlighted by the next lightning strike. Luckily she'd removed her hearing aids. She was terrified of lightning, having been hit twice in the tropics. If she could have managed it, she'd have crawled under her bed, and if the fireworks came any closer, she'd be in bed with me.

"Do you need help getting into your nightie?" I called. The pelting hail created such a racket that I hardly heard her response. "I guess that's a 'No'," I said. I knew my proper Bostonian mother well. Unless she was in a coma, she'd change her own clothes no matter how long that took.

Might the storm be seen as a metaphor for the conflict between our personalities? As Nana aged and became less able. She'd often exhausted my patience. In between our mini-clashes, ennui fuelled my angst. While we'd always had a respectful relationship, I'd received more demonstrative affection from my unmarried aunt.

Then came another one of those darn phone calls. "Hello there, Ms. Clark."

"Do I know you?"

"I called before. Our great offer is still available."

I was silent.

"You know, that free dance lesson."

Pushy, pushy, pushy. "I'm not interested; don't want it even if it is free." *Nothing's free, don't you know.*

The following evening the ringing of the phone once more whipped through the tedious twilight.

"Hi. Your friendly telemarketer here."

I almost dropped the receiver in exasperation.

"Wait, wait. Hear me out. C'mon. You know you're interested."

Now, he's psychic as well as irritating. "Wrong. Look, whoever you are..."

"My name is Harry. Help me out here. Take one lesson, just one," he went on in a syrupy tone. "What have you got to lose? C'mon. Thirty minutes. What's thirty minutes?"

"Okay, okay." I'm such a sucker. "One o'clock next Wednesday, my day off."

"One o'clock it is. Thank you, Miss."

Maybe the Miss got to me because I replaced the phone more gently this time.

Truly, you are crazy, Althea Bryant Clark. As I circled the appointment on my Audubon calendar, I snapped off the tip of my pencil.

4

Suckerrr!!

SOUTHERN CALIFORNIA SWELTERED that January. Even with the Camry's air conditioner on snow-maker, my hands slipped around the steering wheel as I drove the eight miles to the dance studio. *It's not just the heat, fool. You're scared. Admit it. This is the dumbest thing you've ever done.* I swung my Toyota into the shaded parking lot at the back of the building housing the dance studio and peeled my frumpy, dumpy self off the fake leather car seats.

Hot-footing it across the asphalt to the studio's rear door, I touched the brass doorknob. Fire radiated through my fingertips. My hand, with a mind of its own, turned the handle. I urged my trembling legs into a huge air-conditioned room. The sign on the back of the door stated, "Maximum Occupancy: 120," but I saw only one couple undulating to sensuous music, checking themselves in the mirrored walls with every movement.

Now what do I do? I gathered courage and walked a few steps toward the receptionist seated at a desk near the front door. No one paid any attention to me. Skirting the perimeter, I closed in on a Betty Boop look-alike snapping magazine pages, three to the second. "Ahem."

She looked up reluctantly. "Yes?"

I pointed to a square on the large desk calendar in front of her. "I'm Thea Clark, here for a free half hour lesson."

Her eyes traveled down my chunky body to my Cuban-heel pumps. A fake smile appeared on her frosted lips. "One o'clock with Michael Jensen. He'll be here soon." Tipping her head toward a corner of the room where floor-to-ceiling windows met each other, she indicated old-fashioned ice cream parlor chairs. "You may sit there. You can put on your dance shoes while you wait, if you brought them."

"The man on the phone didn't say anything about special shoes," I said.

She shrugged. A looky-loo, not a serious customer, her expression seemed to say.

"I always pictured a dance studio filled with music and dancers," I said. "Where is everybody?"

She dog-eared the corner of her page. "Most of the people who practice here are at a competition in Las Vegas."

By the trimness of her shape, the self-confident B.B. clone was probably a dancer herself.

I pulled myself up to my full five-foot-four, took a deep breath, headed toward the ice cream parlor table near the window and sat, demurely pulling my denim skirt to cover my knees.

Suddenly a white Pinto pulled up at the curb within a few feet of where I waited inside. The six-foot-tall driver climbed out, flattening himself against his vehicle to avoid being hit by fast travelling traffic. He looked to be twenty-something.

Rounding the rear of his car, he reached into the passenger side and removed a black sports bag. Then, up the front door steps he loped. Now inside the double doors, he stopped at Betty B's desk and smiled.

"Hi, Michael," she said returning his grin. Pointing in my direction, she said, "Your freebie is here."

He glanced in my direction.

Hot damn! He's young enough to be my grandson. His hair, that hair! Dyed florescent red and lacquered to stick up like a porcupine's spines. A blazing white Western-style shirt emphasized his broad shoulders, a silver bolo adorned with a turquoise stone took the place of a tie.

His posture was as straight and flat as a T-Square. Dropping his soft leather bag on the floor, he said, "Hi. I'm Michael Jensen," in a drawl matching his Western attire. His handshake was cool and firm. He pulled out his chair noiselessly and sat opposite.

I sized up his luggage and said, "Traveling?"

"My dance bag. Indispensable for a dancer." He unzipped the sports-type bag and withdrew a pair of well-scuffed soft black leather shoes then removed his polished cowboy boots, setting them under the table. His dance shoes tied, he stood, shook his trouser legs, smoothing those immaculate white jeans. Extending his right hand in invitation, he said, "Mrs. Clark. Or, may I call you, Miss Thea?"

Miss Thea!

A small frisson of excitement vibrated all my chakras, as my yoga teacher would say. I felt like young Forrest Gump when he began to run and the braces flew off his legs. My boring present retreated.

"Have you done much ballroom dancing?" he asked.

It had been some time since a male voice tiptoed up my spine. I shrugged. "The Twist and, well, The Swim. That was in the sixties."

Those wide shoulders twitched.

Why can't I say something brilliant? "I confess. I did the mandatory ballroom stuff in the eighth grade during P.E. I really hated those weekly dances in the school cafeteria. I was a shy, size fourteen, self-conscious kid, hiding in the shadows of the more popular girls."

He looked sympathetic. "Yeah. I remember junior high, a real identity crisis time." He turned me to face him. I stepped into his arms. Then he winked; his glinting amber eyes were fringed by lashes so long they looked fake.

My heart beat faster. I moaned, silently of course. He had one of those grins that wrap you up in a hug.

I giggled out loud. *Stop that, you old fool.*

"Sorry?" He chuckled. "Okaay. Do you remember the waltz box step?"

We rounded the floor several times counter-clockwise. "See?" he said. "You're doing fine. Let's try a rumba. The beat is slow, quick, quick, slow." He demonstrated and we practiced together. "Hey. You got it."

Gosh, this is easier than I thought. He barely touches me but I seem to know what to do. Mmm, and he smells good. What is his cologne, I wonder?

The other couple on the floor signaled Michael that they were changing the music to a swing.

"Let's try a swing next," Michael said. "You may know it. I'm sure you did something like it in your day."

He blushed, realizing he'd made a reference to my age. "Well, I mean, some dances don't change much." His red flush deepened.

I grinned. I wasn't offended.

"I can tell that you like swing," he said. "You're more confident." But, a glance at the wall clock and Michael said, "Uh oh, I'm sorry. Your half-hour is over."

Already?

"I hope you enjoyed the lesson enough to come back. Would you like me to make an appointment for you?"

Ah. Here comes the sales pitch.

"I need to think about this."

"Sure," he said. "It's been nice meeting you. I'll walk you to your car."

That's really sweet.

When I was settled in my car, he re-crossed the parking lot to the back door of the studio.

Putting my car in reverse, I checked the rear view mirror. I saw him remove a pack of Marlboros from his shirt pocket and after lighting one, take a deep drag. As I drove out of the lot, he gave me the Queen's wave.

My mind argued with itself on the way home. I felt I was being tempted to do something naughty. I knew my practical-minded mother would disapprove! *It's my own hard-earned money, isn't it?*

The next day at my part-time job as coordinator of a seniors' program, I had little time to dwell on my feelings about the lesson with Mr. Jensen.

A week passed. No one called to sign me up. Now, where was Harry, Telemarketer Extraordinaire?

The half-hour had been more pleasant than I'd anticipated. Just thinking about dancing with Michael put a grin on my face. I wondered how a full hour might make me feel.

What's the danger in one little ol' hour?

Why not try just one?

5

The Road to Oz

"You want to buy one lesson, only one lesson?" asked Betty B. whose real name was Celeste. Scorn came loud and clear over the phone. "We're a franchise. We sell plans."

Like I should know. "I'm not ready for a plan. You may not remember me, I was there two weeks ago for a free half hour lesson with Michael Jensen. Now I'd like to buy a full hour."

Was that a pencil tapping? I could almost hear her frown. She asked, "What's your name again?"

"Clark, Thea."

"Please hold."

I began my own pencil tapping, wondering how they could afford to be so choosy.

"Hello, Mrs. Clark. Are you still there?"

"Yes."

"I'll write you down for one o'clock on Wednesday with Michael."

Shivers traveled up my arms. Abruptly, the Oriental poppy wallpaper appeared to dance across the kitchen walls and I felt a swelling of joy as I whirled on my Nikes.

I'd been nervous and excited on the drive over, wondering if Michael would be as nice as I remembered. Could I last through the longer lesson? I surveyed the large room. *This is more like it.* Six couples sailed around the hardwood floor to Frank Sinatra's "My Funny Valentine." Over the music, I could hear the white noise of the two ceiling fans spinning at full speed. The air was cool, the atmosphere charged with narcissism.

At her desk Celeste flipped through a *Dance Beat* magazine. "Please sign in," she said, handing me a clipboard with that day's appointment sheet attached.

Aha! I'm a paying customer now.

I'd barely sat when Michael said, "Ready? We'll start with the basic steps of the foxtrot." He extended his hand.

Up I jumped, eager to dance to Ol' Blue Eyes and "I've Got You Under My Skin." Tall, slender couples with the set facial expressions of window display mannequins sped past us. The women with beautifully sculpted arms, the men with tight muscular butts.

Focusing on his instructions, I stopped watching the clock. When I'd taught junior high, my fifty-eight minute hour was divided into multi-tasking. Today, following one lousy direction took all my concentration. Twenty-five minutes non-stop and I was out of breath. "I didn't know ballroom dancing took so much energy. These folks make it look so easy."

Michael pointed toward our table. "Let's take a water break, or would you prefer coffee?"

"Water'll be fine, thank you." Glad for the breather,

I dropped into my chair and closed my eyes, opening them when I heard Michael return. I saw he held a cup of water for me and a coffee refill for himself.

"Ready to continue?" he asked.

I nodded. "My mouth's so dry. Why is that?"

"Breathe through your nose more." His voice became crisp. "To finish for today, let's try a waltz with the box step, a promenade, and an underarm turn."

Oh, I like this. Feels like flying.

"Keep your back straight," Michael said. "Stretch your neck up, keep your chin parallel to the floor. This is called your frame."

I can't remember all that. Oh, won't matter. This is my first and last lesson. Sadness engulfed me as those words echoed in my head. *But how can I miss something I've never had?*

Then Michael came to an abrupt stop. Sounding apologetic, he said, "I'm sorry, but your hour is over."

"Really?" I was genuinely surprised. Still holding my hand, he walked me back to the familiar ice cream parlor table and pulled out my chair.

He took a sip of his coffee. "What would you like to do now?"

I stammered. "I—I'm not sure. I don't really have a reason to take private lessons."

He sat back in his chair. I noticed he never slumped. He was silent. *He's quite good looking with his sharply defined cheeks and golden brown eyes.* "The manager can show you some options," he said finally.

Lively music and more dancers filled the building, gyrating to a high energy beat. Others seated at the tiny tables tapped their feet while they chatted. The ever-present mirrors on two walls reflected a crowd.

I like being here.

"The manager is Mr. Allen. His office is in that corner." Michael indicated a door at the far end of the room. "Why don't you talk with him?"

Why not?

My heart pounding with every footfall, I approached the tiny office. I heard a "Come in," when I knocked.

Mr. Allen stood and indicated the only other chair. "Did you enjoy your first lesson?"

"Yes, very much. But before I take more, I need to hear about the fees."

He was the height of Michael, but fifteen pounds heavier with straight black hair and a tanning booth complexion.

Gazing out the window, I breathed deeply to calm the fluttering in my stomach. Outside, all traffic appeared to be going toward a definite destination. *Am I headed anywhere in particular—or am I strolling aimlessly along the shoulder of the road, a bored and lonely observer?*

Mr. Allen interrupted my reverie. "Here are three plans and their costs. Which one might you be interested in?"

I pointed at one set of numbers. "That could be manageable." Barely. My stomach made protest noises.

"All right," he said. "That one includes one group lesson per week, four private lessons per month, and four practice parties."

"What are practice parties?"

"A weekly Friday night dance. To learn to follow different partners, you know."

I stared at the figure on the paper. *Two hundred and ten dollars per month. Why, that's a whole car payment!* My stomach constricted; I clenched my jaw. Yet again, my hands seemed to belong to someone else as they fumbled for my checkbook.

The manager remained silent.

He's not as courtly as Michael. I don't think I'd like him for my teacher. My penmanship was almost illegible from the shaking of my hand as I wrote the check. *What will Old Trout say?*

I was about to hand Mr. Allen my check, when I blurted, "I'd like Michael to be my teacher."

Mr. Allen frowned, withdrawing his hand abruptly. "I choose the teacher for beginners."

It was my turn to pull back my hand.

I could see him repress a sigh as he examined the large plastic calendar in front of him. He nodded, and not very graciously, I thought. "Okay, Mr. Jensen it is."

Once outside his office, my heart beating on high, I waved at Michael, the plan's receipt in my hand. He sat with a young blonde, an Alice in Wonderland look-alike.

"Excuse me, Michael." I included Alice in my smile. "I've signed up for a month beginning next week."

He stood. "Great," he said and offered that special "only-for-you" grin. "Could you buy a pair of dance shoes by your next lesson? You'll learn so much faster with the proper shoes."

Studying my feet, I asked, "These pumps aren't suitable?"

"Street shoes are too slippery. Dance shoes have suede soles." He grabbed a piece of scrap paper on which he wrote an address. "There's a specialty store not far from here."

"How much would such shoes cost?" I asked innocently.

"Sometimes you can get them on sale. Usually, they're about a hundred dollars."

Whoosh, said my checkbook—again, desperately trying to clamp itself shut.

6

If I Weren't So Old and Straight

BRIGHT SUNSHINE had replaced the shade in the parking lot, turning my pale blue Camry into a silver chariot. I sat with the driver's side door open, feeling heat waves wash over me as they streamed from the vehicle.

Now, you've torn it. Where's your sales resistance? How will you explain dance lessons to Nana? Mentally, I knew I could go back inside and retrieve my check. I also knew I had time that afternoon to check out the shoe store. *Why not? I dare you, Miss Thea.* And I pointed the car toward the Harbor Freeway.

Finding the store was easy. Deciding which pair to buy was not. No sparkly red shoes like Dorothy's could I see, but instead a pair of white leather, open-toed two inch sandals was on sale. Outside, I saw no rainbow, but heard a faint whisper: "Follow the yellow brick road. Follow the yellow brick road." *Where? Have a little imagination, Thea. Shut up and follow the damn road.*

At home, I cautiously slid the patio door aside. The house was silent. I felt like an errant teenager sneaking upstairs, past the creaking step on the landing. I peeked into the dragon's den and found her asleep in her recliner warmed by the late afternoon sun. Good. I'll pretend I've been home all along.

My mother owned the publishing rights to the book of Thea. For once, I wanted to include a chapter she'd not read.

"I don't see Michael," I said, standing at Celeste's desk. "Am I here at the right time?" I knew that I was. I had a thing about punctuality.

She ceased honing her talons. "You're his first lesson of the afternoon. He'll be here. Why not put on your shoes?" She eyed the dark blue box with approval then returned to her manicure.

Carrying the precious cargo to my usual table, I placed it lovingly on the faux marble top, lifted the lid and peeked inside. The pristine white leather shoes costing seventy-five dollars lay gently nestled in dove gray tissue. Separating the layers I encountered a fragrance not often present with today's plastic composition shoes, the unique aroma of genuine leather. I turned over one shoe to caress the suede sole. Eventually, with both shoes buckled, I took tentative steps on the smooth carpet. I'd never had new shoes feel so comforting. Placing one foot, heel to toe on the highly polished wood, I suddenly jerked myself backward to avoid a tall couple whirling by. I imagined the pair as Fred Astaire and Ginger Rogers, beckoning me to dance a threesome with them. Why had I waited so long to feel this kind of joy?

My fantasy bubble popped as I heard Michael say, "Now, you're serious." I hadn't seen him come in the front door. His drawl slithered up my spine. All in white as usual except for his cowboy boots. He gracefully sat.

"About what?" I asked.

"Dancing, of course." He bent to remove the boots. "Dance shoes are expensive." Straightening, he shook his ironed jeans back into place. "You have to take good care of them so they'll last. Never wear them on the street."

"Never?"

"Junk, old gum, oil in parking lots, water and mud puddles—all ruin the suede soles."

"When I'm good to them, they'll be good to me?"

"You got it."

I scanned the room. "Lots more people here this week."

"Last week, several of our couples went to comps. There is at least one every month somewhere in the U.S."

Still having no interest in the competitive dance world, I didn't pursue the subject. "What do we do today?"

"First, how about reviewing last week?" He released that sweet smile.

"I hate to admit it but I've already forgotten what that was." I grimaced. "Is that true of all beginners, or just seniors?"

"Not unusual for anybody. You'll soon lock the steps into your muscle memory." His amber eyes grew serious. "Give yourself time."

Oh, if you weren't so young and gay!
Damn! If I weren't so old and straight.

7

Just Use Your Other Left Foot

"Michael, I'm embarrassed to ask you to repeat your instructions. It bothers me that I can't handle more than one at a time."

He'd just finished teaching me four basic steps of the cha cha. The studio was filled with professional dancers rehearsing for a showcase. Distracted by so many people, I was only half-heartedly listening to him.

"Why can't I coordinate my body parts, especially my feet? You tell me to step on my right and what do I do? I step on my left, and then I tangle with your feet. Oops! Like now."

"Not a big deal," said Michael. He squeezed my hand. "Soon, like I said, your muscle memory will kick in and most moves will become automatic, like driving your car."

My muscle memory must have Alzheimer's today.

"But you do have to focus on me. I won't bump into anyone or let them collide with you." He moved me around the floor in sync with the others. "And, Miss Thea, don't think so hard. Just use your other left foot when I say 'change weight'."

My other left foot!

I laughed but then a minor miracle happened. I don't know why those silly instructions worked, but they did. I'd simply gotten confused and lost track of where my weight was supposed to be.

From then on, whenever he said, "No, your *other* left foot," I just switched feet, automatically shifting weight.

No problemo.

"You ready?" asked Michael the next afternoon when I hadn't moved out of my chair.

"Everybody here is probably wondering what business this old lady has taking up space alongside these elegant young professionals."

"Not so. First, the pros only watch themselves in the mirrors. Believe me, you don't exist except as an obstacle to avoid."

"Oh."

He flapped his lashes. Mesmerized, I walked into his arms.

The following week, I watched Michael teaching 'Alice.' He nodded when I walked past the two of them rumbaing. Escorting her off the floor as the music died away, he patted her shoulder, "Good job, today."

I noticed she put her arm around his waist and gave him a hug. When the two sat down to rest, he asked me, "Why weren't you at the practice party last Friday?"

I shrugged. "Everyone knows everyone else. I only know you. I don't want to sit on the sidelines like a wallflower."

"Like a what?"

"Oh, never mind."

"Miss Thea," said Michael patiently, "You've paid for these parties."

"I don't want to dance with other people. I only want to dance with you." I sounded like a petulant junior high kid. "The minute I make a mistake," I continued, "my partner would know I'm a beginner."

He snorted. "But you *are* a beginner! Everybody's a beginner sometime, even the pros."

The dance lessons filled a social void in my life. While I loved my job coordinating classes and events for seniors, the dance lessons focused on me. Michael's courtliness pleased me. That hour with him became a beauty mark on the face of my work-week.

Up to now, our conversations had been limited to dance talk, but as the weeks flowed by, we brought up personal issues. I discussed my teenaged grandson, Luke, now living with Nana and me, and Michael related how he had run away from home at an early age.

One day he surprised me with, "Did you know," he opened wide those golden topaz eyes, "that a beautiful young woman back East had a crush on me?"

I grinned. "You're very charming and mighty cute. But surely she knew you were gay."

He shrugged. "I never said anything to her one way or the other. Did you know when I first met you?"

I swallowed a sarcastic reply. "You mean, you led her on?"

He winked. *Ooh! I wish I could flap my eyelashes like that.*

The next Friday at nine o'clock, wearing my favorite split skirt with a long-sleeved black turtleneck top, I drove to the party. I left Nana in bed, knowing that she'd sleep for at least four hours, so I wouldn't have to explain my absence. Luke was playing video games in his bedroom, and he knew how to reach me in an emergency.

Once inside I searched the studio for Michael among all the others chatting around the perimeter of the dance floor, waiting for the music to begin.

I don't see him. He's not here. I'm not going to stay.

Across the room the lovely young lady I'd dubbed Alice waved me over to her table. "You know, he's required to be here," she said, reading the worry on my face and dejection in my body language. Reluctantly, I sat next to her, fully aware that by contrast she was half my age and a quarter my size.

"Even if he doesn't come," she went on, "the other teachers will dance with you." She flipped her long blonde hair. "Get ready. Change your shoes."

Oh, the confidence of the young and pretty.

I was buckling my left shoe when I heard Michael's familiar, "Hi, y'all. How's everybody doin'?" His drawl accented his country Western apparel, and tonight he wore a Western straw hat.

My heart beat faster; maybe I even blushed. I took a deep breath. My security blanket had arrived.

"You're my first dance partner, Podner," Michael said.

Giving him my best Scarlet O'Hara smile, I said, "Yea-us, Suh."

We danced a slow rumba then the music changed to a foxtrot. He thanked me and escorted me to the table, then invited Alice, the lovely Miss Wonderland, to dance.

I was beginning to feel conspicuously alone when a gray-haired gentleman I'd not seen at the studio stood at my right, holding out his hand.

"May I have this dance?" he said.

Relieved to join the group on the floor I rose, flicked my skirt, and bolstered my shrinking ego. Facing him in dance position, I hoped he wouldn't sense my apprehension.

Damn! When he moved forward, we immediately collided. He tried again. But now I was flustered.

Double damn!

He apologized.

"I'm still a beginner," I muttered as if my toe mashing hadn't already revealed that.

"You'll get better with practice," he said politely, and when the music stopped, returned me to my table. I noticed he didn't ask me to dance again.

Will I sit out dance after dance, all by myself? Shades of those embarrassing days in the junior high cafeteria.

"Hello." Michael was standing across from me with a cup of coffee. "May I get one for you?"

"No, thanks. I only drink tea."

"Oh, well, then. Let's dance. This one's a waltz, your favorite."

Look out, y'all. Here I come! The one-two-three beat swept me joyously around the floor.

Michael grinned. "You really are happy waltzing, aren't you?"

I beamed under the umbrella of his smile.

All week long I debated the expense versus the ego-boosting satisfaction. *Face it, Thea. Michael makes you feel like an attractive woman again.*

The days between Wednesdays dragged. I liked my job, but I was beginning to love dancing more. However, I thought adding a second private lesson might bankrupt me.

One day Michael frowned and tilted his head. "Miss Thea, your month is over."

My stomach churned. *No! I don't want to end this adventure. But am I treading troubled water? I'm developing an attachment to him.* Then, I figured, the hell with it. I could always give up eating. I searched in my purse for my checkbook and with a rapidly-beating heart hurried to the manager's office to pay for a three-month plan.

What would Nana say when she saw that check on the bank statement? *I need to confess my secret life before budget time.*

8

A Secret Life

"When did you begin dancing?" I asked Michael when we took a break from a fast samba.

He gazed past my head to some distant place. "At eight, I was always leaping around the house, so a friend suggested ballet lessons to my mother. She was glad to have me leap someplace else."

I tried to imagine his mother's thoughts regarding a young son who wanted to dance ballet.

"Michael." I paused to change the subject. "Today I paid for a three months' plan."

The lines around his mouth penciled in a smile. As his beam reached full wattage, he squeezed my arm. "Okay." Then, he grew serious.

Now what?

"Can you stay a few minutes now to talk?"

I dreaded learning anything about his private life. I'd overheard one of his students mention his name in the same paragraph with pneumonia. Because I knew Michael was gay, I followed the publicity about AIDS. I grew uneasy.

"Nothing bad," he hurried to say. Then, "Do you know what a Team Match is?"

I finished changing into street shoes and sat back in my

chair to give him my full attention. "Sounds like a sporting event."

"Close. It's a fun contest between local studios."

I hadn't been tempted to participate in any of the out-of-town competitions the studio advertised, but a small intramural event sounded intriguing. "Does it cost anything?"

"Oh, yes. This is one way studios make money. Students pay an overall fee to enter, then moderate fees for every dance, or heat."

This hobby is a money pit. "I don't know, Michael. I've never been in a dance contest. Don't you think I might be too old?"

He was silent. Was he going for the politically correct answer? He seemed to make up his mind. "Each heat is ninety seconds. Hey, you dance longer than that during your lesson."

"It's the competing part. I'm not sure I have the chutzpah." Then, I chuckled. "I do recall a swim meet at the local pool. I had polio as a toddler, so my mother enrolled me in swim classes wherever we moved. It was her idea of hydrotherapy."

"I would have never known you'd had polio. I'm not even sure what it is."

"Mine was a light case of paralysis. My right side was stronger than my left and I tended to swim in circles. But swimming in a straight line mattered a lot when I was eight and entered in that meet." I smiled with the memory, and found the smells were still surprisingly vivid: the sharp tang of the disinfectant used in the hospital-green tile showers, the rubber of the bathing caps, and the wool of the pre-1950s bathing suits.

I remember how I waited for my turn, sitting on a sodden wood bench against the green and beige tiled wall of the Olympic-sized pool. I watched the older girls line up, dive in, and swim to the opposite side. Mothers, including my own, hovered nearby with dry towels and ladylike encouragement.

Now I glanced out the studio window at the traffic, making a face. "When I was told to line up on the pool's edge, I saw I was the shortest and youngest. By mistake my name had been listed with the twelve-to-fourteen-year olds."

On your mark, get set, *go*! said the swim coach.

"I did my best, but I came in last. Everyone clapped, in relief, I think, when I finally reached the opposite end of the pool. But the next moment remains forever with me, the feeling of achievement when the judge awarded me an Honorable Mention just for finishing."

I told Michael how the local paper's photographer took my picture. I still have the clipping with the headline, "An Olympic-sized Heart Gets Honorable Mention."

Michael smiled. "Traveling in circles is helpful in dancing."

"Thanks. But tell me more about the Team Match."

"It's pretty basic," he said. "Students with their teachers compete against students from other studios. You'd be in Newcomers or maybe even Beginners."

"What do you mean, *or*?"

"Newcomers don't have to wear a costume. Beginners do."

"When does this happen?"

"Three weeks from Friday."

"Three weeks!"

"Don't look so shocked," he said. "You only dance the steps you already know."

"Thank goodness for that."

"Unless, of course, you'd like to take some extra lessons. But," he hurried to add, "you don't have to. "You do need a dress with a full skirt," he made a circular gesture as he spoke, "one that will ripple outwards as you turn." He scrutinized my head. "And your hair should be fixed in a pony tail or a French roll so it's contained and neat."

I squished my mousy brown shoulder-length tresses into a ponytail.

"That's it," he said. "Judges like to see a clean line from the back of your neck to your shoulders. Adds to the overall look of your frame."

Oh, frame again! Do I have to buy new shoes?"

"No. Your white ones are fine."

Thank goodness. And thank goodness Nana was slowly letting go of the banking. "I don't want to balance the statement anymore," she'd said. "Too hard for me to read it." Her glaucoma worsened. I felt bad about that but was glad I didn't have to explain the checks for dance lessons. I wasn't ready to reveal my secret hobby.

Leaving the studio, I headed for the nearby mall, determined to buy a dress he'd described for a price I could afford.

An hour later, I took home a pale pink size twelve with three quarter length sleeves and an A-shape skirt. Quickly hiding the shopping bag in my closet, I checked to see if my mother was awake. Time to tell Nana what I'm doing. Why not? I asked myself. I'd been my mother's work in progress for sixty-two years, married or unmarried. *This is one time I don't want her looking over my shoulder and offering caustic remarks. This adventure is still too precious and too fragile.*

9

Now, I'm a Ballroom Mom

THREE WEEKS LATER I drove to the studio, my new dress carefully reposing in its garment bag on the back seat. For the first time, the parking lot was almost full; I was lucky to find a space. *Am I late? Of course not. I'm never late.*

Everyone was early.

Inside the studio, I found it transformed by the maximum capacity crowd, some sitting in chairs lining the walls, others milling and chatting, the noise level reflecting the excitement of the event. Opening the door to the small dressing room, I found several women changing from their street clothes into bejeweled gowns.

A glamorous blonde in a bright yellow satin formal, the bodice fish-scaled with sequins, the skirt hemmed in Big Bird feathers, smiled. "Hi, I'm Patty. We've all been beginners. We know those first-time jitters. Let's see what you brought." She took the bag from me and unzipped it with a quick pull of her yellow acrylic nails. "Hmm. Very sweet." Handing me the pink rayon dress she said, "Just get out there and have a good time."

Easy for you to say.

"Thank you," I said. "I appreciate encouragement, coming from one who looks so beautiful."

She smiled and made a dismissive gesture.

Dressed and primped to their satisfaction, all but one of the dancers exited to the dance floor. "Break a leg!" called Gorgeous Yellow as she carefully closed the door.

Break a leg. What a bizarre thing to say to a dancer!

A shapely brunette approved herself in the long mirror on the back of the closed door. She twitched her brief white satin skirt and fluffed the fringe on her bikini top. "I'm dancing only Latin today, no smooth. What heats are you doing?"

"The waltz, foxtrot, tango, then, East Coast swing and rumba."

"Well, break a leg." She laughed. "Better break both with all those heats." She opened the door that led directly onto the dance floor and samba-ed away. Suddenly, the dressing room felt sucked of all excitement and energy.

I twirled once in front of the mirror then I, too, opened the door to a ballroom vibrating with laughter and music. Scanning around, I saw Michael seated directly across from where I stood. He was talking with another man his height, dressed as was Michael in a black turtleneck and black dress pants.

Music buoys my spirits, makes me cry, makes me want to fly. I smiled.

Noticing me, he waved and the two men ambled across the floor to greet me. "Thea, this is Don from a studio down south. We'll be dancing against one of his ladies. And winning, won't we?" He gave me a Tom Cruise grin, a lift of his eyebrows, then took my hand to turn me around to see how the skirt swirled. "Perfect," he pronounced. "And your hair looks great. Wear it like that tonight at the practice party."

"Tonight?" I squeaked.

"The dance party. You're coming, of course. To tell everyone about the Team Match."

"What if I don't do very well?"

"Miss Thea. We all know this is your first time. Lighten up."

Break a leg. Lighten up. Have fun. Whooee.

Mr. Allen, the manager, wearing attire similar to Michael's, quieted the music, tapped the microphone and welcomed everyone.

People who'd paid to watch drifted toward the rows of chairs against the front and side windows. Michael escorted me to a group of chairs to join other members of our team. Taking my right hand, he said, "You're cold. Shake your hands and arms to loosen up. This is going to be fun!"

Riiiight! But the Hokey Pokey didn't do the trick. *Lord! Why am I here?*

Michael broke into my anxiety attack. "Pin this on my shirt, please." He handed me a sheet of white paper with Number 15 hand-lettered in black marker.

Hyper with excitement, he flexed his feet, marching in place. He reminded me of a colt at his maiden race, flaring nostrils, fired up ready to burst through the starting gate.

"Stand still," I commanded. "Or I'll stick you with this safety pin."

"We're the first group to compete," he said. "Don't sit

down. We'll line up over there by the dressing room door."

He took my hand in an iron grip. I wasn't going anywhere unless I fainted. Waiting for the music to start, I stared straight ahead to the hurrying traffic outside. How could the people in their cars not be aware of the excitement and tension filling the studio? Snapping out of my reverie, I realized Michael was moving me around the perimeter of the room using the basic waltz step. *One*, two, three; *one*, two, three.

Oh, lovely. I like this.

Suddenly I heard someone shout, "Go, 15!" I turned my head to find the caller.

"Don't do that!" Michael hissed. "Don't let yourself be distracted by anything. Focus on me!"

He hadn't warned me about the jocular yelling from the sidelines, or how the teachers teased each other with personal remarks. As we danced past Don, he held up a hand-made sign, "Hey, Dude, your zipper's slipping." Michael neither turned his head nor missed a step.

For heaven's sake. It's like my grandson's Little League.

When I wasn't dancing, I, too, yelled for my team-mates. "Go for it, Patty! Looking good, Linda!"

Gosh, I've become a Ballroom Mom.

The Newcomer's waltz heat followed the other smooth heats: foxtrot and tango. Without resting, I repeated the three dances as a Beginner as well as a Newcomer. We didn't even leave the floor, standing where we ended the last dance.

Michael said, "You'll do both Newcomers' and Beginners'

cha cha, rumba, and merengue."

"Whew. And then, we're done?"

"Yes. Then, you're free to have refreshments, talk with friends, or cheer others from our studio."

Michael escorted me to my seat in the front row. He didn't stay, but took Alice to the floor for her smooth heats.

She's really good.

When they finished Intermediate waltz and tango, she plopped into her chair dabbing at the perspiration on her forehead. She wore a blue satin dress with one-inch feathers around the hem and over her shoulders. It reminded me of the old song my mother sang to me at bedtime, "In her sweet little Alice blue gown." My mother had wanted to be a singer. Sadly, she was disappointed in that too.

Looking directly at me, Michael asked, "Did you invite friends or relatives?"

I shook my head.

"How come?"

"I wasn't going to ask anyone to pay money to see me embarrass myself."

"You've done great so far."

"Mostly seconds and thirds and there were only three of us competing."

"You got a First in the tango."

"Yay. I felt giddy when she handed me that First Place ribbon. You know, I wasn't prepared for how I'd feel. I wanted to hug her. I guess you don't do that to a judge."

"Uh, no."

"I'm disappointed by the Third Places. I must have deserved them, but still . . ."

Mr. Allen at the microphone called for Beginners and their teachers to move onto the floor.

"Let's go," said Michael holding out his hand. "Feel the music. Stay focused on me."

I hope Michael can't tell how nervous I am. I'm scared to death I'll step on him or get in his way. Of course he knows. Dancers read body language better than politicians.

Twenty minutes later, after we'd finished the rumba, cha cha, merengue and a swing, Michael said, "See, that wasn't so bad."

I gave him a hesitant smile.

"Both your swing and merengue were good. A little more hip motion in the rumba and you'll get a First next time."

Hip motion? I'd spent years trying to camouflage my wide hips. Now, he wants me to flaunt them.

Next time? What next time?

My eyes roved the large space filled with spectators on two sides and competitors everywhere. People laughing, chatting, calling out to their friends, and music in "surround" sound. I like this. I like being scared, pretending I'm not. *I like being in Michael's arms. I love this energy.*

Finally, all the heats were over; all the ribbons awarded. The audience signaled an end to the afternoon by consuming the remaining refreshments and congratulating their dancing friends. Michael's energy soared and he excused himself to socialize with teachers from the other studio.

He could still prance but I was danced out. My hips were sore. But I had done better than I expected. I'd won a First in a tango, three seconds and two thirds in the Smooths.

I drove home in my plain peppermint pink rayon dress singing, "Zippety Do Dah." Perspiration had eroded my Cover Girl foundation, leaving my cheeks in stripes. My ponytail was in disarray, much of the hair having escaped from the banana clip. But, oh, what a marvelous time!

At home and sound asleep, Nana was unaware that I'd been gone. I made myself a cup of tea, changed into slacks, and sat on my bed to read a Robert Parker mystery. Though I stared at the printed words, I had little idea of their meaning. Instead, I relived the colors, music, and the excitement of an afternoon such as I'd never experienced. I glanced at the ribbons I'd dropped on my bureau and felt a twinge of sadness that my mother wouldn't, couldn't, see them.

Hey. The practice party starts at nine. I can still shower, change, eat, and get there.

10

Michael's Health Problems Escalate

Thus, in my sixties, I tapped into a remote corner of my psyche where a life-long desire to dance had crouched, waiting. Michael's courtesy and patience overcame my initial shyness. I found him charming and I responded like a late-blooming rose in the summer sunshine.

But events wilted that bloom and dimmed the sunlight. Michael's health problems escalated. Now, I rode a bucking bronco of hope and depression. Though I had a standing appointment on Wednesday afternoons, he didn't always show. Nor would he call me to cancel. Anxiously, I'd look for his car in the lot, relieved when I saw the white Pinto, frustrated when I didn't.

One Wednesday when I arrived again to discover he was a no-show, I stormed over to Miss Celeste's desk. "Does anyone know where Michael is? I'm supposed to have a lesson."

She frowned. "Didn't anyone call you? He's in the hospital. Pneumonia."

Ashamed of my tantrum, I mumbled, "I'm sorry." Still, I felt taken for granted. Surely, I deserved the courtesy of a phone call. "Didn't Michael have pneumonia awhile ago?"

She fidgeted, then shrugged.

The anti-fraternization policy of the studio limited what

I could do. An atmosphere of secrecy grew around him. Others at the studio responded to my questions with silence.

At the Friday parties I'd watched him closely when he danced with his other students. He didn't seem any less energetic than the rest of the teachers and he usually walked off the floor with a bounce in his step. Perplexed, I guessed I was worrying needlessly.

A few days later, he phoned. He'd never before called me at home.

"Do you have a minute?" he asked.

"Sure."

"I've something important to tell you." He paused. I could hear an intake of breath or maybe he was taking a drag on one of his ever-present Marlboros. "I want to give you a choice whether or not to continue dancing with me."

What?

He rushed on, "I'm HIV Positive. You know what that means?" He waited for an answer.

I bit my lip. Too stunned.

He continued. "I've known for some time."

Shoot. How come I'm not trusted? What am I, chopped liver? The ice water of reality rushed down my veins. "Did you know this when I began lessons with you?"

"Yes."

Anger, despair, sadness, regret, and anxiety fought for dominance. I gritted my teeth, clamped my jaws shut. I didn't want to blurt out something inappropriate. I was truly sorry about his situation, but I also had concern for my own. "Michael, I'm not sure I understand what being HIV positive means in your case. And, sorry to sound so selfish, but should I be worried about myself?"

The other end of the phone was silent.

"Do any of your other students know?"

"No. And when I tell the management, I'll be fired."

God! What a mess!

I'd practiced how I might respond if he brought up the subject. But now that the moment had arrived, my rehearsed phrases failed to materialize.

"I'm sorry, really sorry, Michael. I don't know what to say."

"That's okay. If you want to continue, call me at home but not at the studio. I'll have to find another studio that won't know about me."

Whoa. How much more is he not telling me?

"Thank you, Michael," saying his name into the phone softly, "for being up front with me. Not all that easy to do, I suspect." I became even quieter. I wasn't sure where the conversation should go next. He was not one to encourage expressions of feelings. While we'd talked some about our lives away from the studio, he'd maintained a reserve I respected.

He went on, "You know, the studio discourages friendships between teachers and students. I've actually told you more about my life than I should have. Right now, I'm not quite sure who my friends are."

Practical me said, "Don't you have a contract?"

"In this case that won't make any difference."

I was indignant. "I'll stand by you if you want go to the manager."

He sighed, "Thea, you really don't get it."

"What don't I get?"

"It's over. My professional life is over." He sounded as though he spoke through clenched teeth. "You have no idea what it's like to be gay right now. Being HIV positive is a death sentence."

I wanted so much to reassure him with a hug, but instead I said, "To be honest, after you had pneumonia I felt uneasy. I waited for you to bring up your health. I asked my friend the Chinese medicine specialist about safety."

Simple precautions, Thea, are all that's needed, she'd said.

"You never said anything. Why didn't you just ask me?" He sounded impatient and cross, unusual for him.

"I didn't want to pry. I was reluctant to ask you about a personal issue. This is your business, yet with all the emotionally-charged publicity about AIDS, I've been nervous, very nervous." I sighed. "And, I felt if you cared enough about me, you'd tell me what was going on."

I heard him take a deep breath, then exhale.

"Michael, please, believe me, I am your friend. I appreciate the kindness you've shown me and I'll help where I can. And be assured that I want to continue lessons with you as long as you want to teach. I'm relieved that you've brought this into the open."

Still I felt gut-punched. *Life without my lessons will be devoid of joy.*

"Were you worried that I'd be afraid of getting AIDS?" I continued. "After all, we're not exchanging body fluids. We're just dancing."

He laughed, "You're not as naive as you look."

Abruptly, I was attacked by a wrenching fear. *How will he support himself? My lesson fees alone won't be enough.*

He interrupted my thoughts, "I like teaching you, Thea. I don't want to stop. Mornings when my energy is low and it's hard to get out of bed, I remind myself that it's your lesson day. I make myself get dressed and drive to the studio just so I can see your pale blue Camry parked in the shade."

I heard a smile in his voice. "As usual," he said, "you're reading while you wait and when you look up, I see the relief on your face. How can I not do my best for you, at least the best I have that day?"

Then in a whisper, he said, "I'm really sorry about the days I don't show, or even call."

We came to an agreement of sorts. The days he could give me a lesson at another nearby studio he'd phone me before I left for work. I yo-yo'd between hope and despair.

11

When Does Two Become One

THE STUDIO WAS STILL the focus of my leisure. One day on the phone Michael asked, "Have you ever gone on the VIP evenings? Dining and dancing at nightclubs?" He paused. "They're not on your monthly plan."

"Don't leave me in suspense."

"A group of us go by limo to a hotel or a restaurant with a dance floor and combo."

"And how much are these evenings?"

"About two hours of private lessons."

"Whoa!"

I could imagine him winking. "This includes your dinner, drinks and, of course, me."

Who wants to stay at home when I can dance with Michael? "Hey, sign me up for the next one."

Two weeks later, the surprise destination was a well-known Wilshire Boulevard hotel. Michael advised, "Buy a new cocktail dress, something that makes you feel like a princess. You deserve it."

Do I? Do I deserve to spend even more money on myself?

I bought a gown of lavender and pale blue chiffon, a many-layered splendored thing that swirled when I twirled. That evening, dressed up in my new finery, I joined others at the studio to ride in a rented limousine, toasting each other with champagne. By the time we arrived at the hotel, I felt quite relaxed.

Michael helped me out of the car. Taking my elbow, he escorted me into the marble, brass and glass foyer bordered by expensive shops. Two window-shopping, spike-heeled women looked Michael over, winked at him and giggled.

"See!" he said. "Not everyone knows I'm gay."

"Michael. Those were ladies of the night. Need I say more?"

We exited the elevator at the top floor, stepping into a black and red plush waiting room hushed except for the melodious harmony of a four-man combo. White Diamonds, Obsession, and Chanel collaged the air, competing with delicious aromas from the gourmet menu.

Our party occupied a large table in one of the corners where the massive windows came together at right angles, overlooking the sparkling city below. I chose Lobster Newberg, and in between courses Michael escorted me to the miniscule floor. I noted the expressions of people we passed.

They're probably thinking, How nice that such a handsome young man is giving his grandmother an evening on the town. Even if they thought he was gigolo, I didn't care. I was dancing in public and loving it. The combo was great, the dinner delectable. The caviar canapes alone were worth the price of my dress.

As a splinter of sunlight expands when a door slowly

opens, Michael's revelations encouraged a more serious level in our relationship. He was a considerate listener when I brought up my own family issues, especially involving Luke, my tall, handsome, rebellious fourteen-year-old grandson. Sympathetic yet neutral, Michael only gave advice when asked.

Ha! I have a therapist packaged as a dance teacher.

"Anytime I can help, Thea, in any way, other than money, of course, you have only to ask."

"Thanks. I do appreciate the offer. I'm supposed to be an expert with adolescents, but..."

Luke had been with us six months and his presence was an irritant to Nana. She wanted to return to our quiet, bland home-life. "You're just a wimp," she said to me one day when Luke was particularly contentious. "Why can't you make him obey?"

I fought back. "Your only experience raising a child was with me, Miss Goody Two Shoes. Why can't I make him obey? That's a good question, for which I have no answer."

I explained my late afternoon and evening absences as going to the movies with friends or working late. It was easy. I only had to cover the Wednesday afternoon lesson, the three hours on Friday nights, and an occasional VIP evening. I did feel guilty about being evasive, but not enough to risk what I thought would be a vitriolic confrontation.

However, I became anxious about this new outlay of

money. Throughout most of my married life everyone else's needs came first. I wasn't accustomed to spending hundreds of dollars on myself. When I wrote the next monthly check, a cramp held my stomach hostage and perspiration trickled down my back.

Michael, being a gay man, complicated any discussion of him. I'd never tested how homophobic my mother might be. I had to admit that having a secret life with a special friend was fun, even risky. But after three V.I.P. evenings, I decided I'd had enough expensive socializing. I settled on one lesson, one group class a week and the Friday night parties. Shy about discussing my dancing, I still hadn't invited my friends.

During the following month, the issue of Michael's health didn't come up and I let go of the worry. One November afternoon he startled me. "Would you like to dance a solo with me at a Christmas benefit?"

"A what?" I stopped drinking the water I'd brought to the table while we were on a break.

"To buy toys for disadvantaged children in Orange County."

I stared at him. "Backtrack a little. What do you mean—a solo?"

"In ballroom dancing a solo is danced by two people. It's only called a solo because no one else is on the floor at the same time."

I sat back, still sipping my drink. "Just the two of us? On

the floor by ourselves? All eyes focused on us?"

"Everyone watched you at the Team Match."

"We weren't dancing alone. Other couples drew attention too."

He laughed. "A solo routine is only three minutes. It's over before you know it." He shrugged. "Just a performance, no judges, no prizes, no pressure."

I hate it when anyone says that. No pressure! Ha. Michael had no idea what nerve I needed to dance in front of an unfamiliar crowd. A solo no less! "Let me think about this. By the way, would it cost anything?"

He chuckled and shrugged. "By now, Miss Thea, you know every event at a studio costs the student. Yes. You pay a fee to be in the program. Extra lessons would be nice too."

I weighed cost versus the pleasure of dancing with Michael. Ten months had gone by since I began lessons with him. I couldn't bear to look into the future. It seemed I was the only one who knew what potential trouble lay ahead.

"Okay, tell me what's required."

"Choose your favorite dance," said Michael.

"Waltz," I blurted.

"You need a dress more elegant than the pink one."

"Hey. I saw what some of the women wore at the Team Match. Those fancy costumes looked expensive. About how much?"

"In the neighborhood of a couple of thousand," he said.

"Holy cannoli! Pretty fancy neighborhood!"

He laughed. "Seriously though, you might find a dressmaker to customize a formal for less."

Is this my last tango?

"I'll consult my checkbook. Say, when is this event?"

"A month from now. And another thing. For a solo, you need your own choreography."

"What do you mean? Don't we just go out there and dance?"

"Oh, no. In a solo, you never just wing it. The whole thing is carefully planned." Michael winked. "Not to worry, the routine is made up from steps familiar to you."

"Do you create this choreography?"

"No. A coach does that."

"A coach? Oh. I get it. How much extra?"

"About double my rate."

"And your regular hourly fee is on top of that?"

He smiled and offered a Gaelic shrug.

Am I being scammed? So what?

Thousands I didn't have. Hundreds I might find.

I opened the Yellow Pages and walked my fingers to the ad of a local dressmaker. The next day, on visiting her shop, I saw displayed several beautiful wedding gowns in various stages of completion. Luckily, I'd brought a sketch of what I wanted.

The petite, dark-haired seamstress looked carefully at my line drawing. "Yes. I can do this."

"Can you suggest where I might buy the fabric?"

She wrote on the sketch an address and a name. "You tell Ali I sent you, and he will give you a good price." Her voice had a musical quality, reminding me of the crystal wind chimes on my grandmother's porch.

In the Thomas Guide, I could see that the store was nestled in a maze of one-way streets in downtown Los Angeles. Exiting the freeway, I encountered construction everywhere. I began to sweat. Soon I was lost. In a panic, I found myself totally turned around. *I'm afraid I've left my sense of direction in my other purse.* Fortunately, a corner gas station appeared on my right.

"Ma'am," said the polite, middle-aged attendant, "you're headed in the wrong direction. Keep on going and you'll end up in Whittier."

Oh, damn!

I wrote his directions on the scrap of paper with my dress sketch while he filled my car with Regular. He tipped his baseball cap, and I drove out of the station heading west. Fifteen minutes later I found the building and parked nervously in a deserted lot around the corner. The shabby two-story structure appeared abandoned; its one large display window was covered with fly-specked and moisture-streaked butcher paper. I checked my scrawled directions again. This was the place.

The door knob didn't turn easily. *Shoot, now what?* I was about to leave when the door finally swung inward. Tentatively stepping across the threshold, I was accosted by a psychedelic array of colors and patterns. Stretched before me was a huge barn-like space filled with tables and counters completely covered with vertical rolls of fabric, a colorful army in repose, ready to march to a Fantasia concerto. The walls lined with shelves up to the ceiling held hundreds of bolts dazzling the eyes with busy patterns and combinations of colors hardly imaginable. The air was dry and musty. From a two-story skylight, the sun's rays fanned out in rainbow-colored dust motes.

A dark-haired, olive-complexioned man with a neatly trimmed mustache walked briskly toward me. He wore his brilliant white shirt open at the neck; his navy blue trousers were pressed to a knife-edge.

"How can I help you?" he asked in the same musical accent I'd heard at the wedding dress shop.

"Darla from South Bay sent me," I said.

"Ahhh."

I showed him my sketch of the simple spaghetti-strapped calf-length dress with a 1950s full skirt. Using hand gestures, I explained how I wanted the skirt to swing and ripple while I turned.

"Ah. Like Ginger Rogers. Lots of theater people buy from us." He gestured toward an archway at the rear of the store. "Follow me, please, to the basement where we keep specialty materials."

I hurried behind him down stairs, through a dark narrow hallway with closed doors on either side. Wouldn't take much to push me inside and lock the door.

Ali checked to see that I followed. He opened a door to our right and pointed to rows of luscious colors, which reminded me of the days when I played with paper dolls, the ever-present girl-toy of my pre-teen years.

My "Originals by Thea" in those days wore Ziegfield Follies costumes made of scraps of fabrics from my home made dresses, found feathers, and sequins. I spent many hours with my dolls, every one with a toothpick glued to her backside so she could be stuck vertically in the holes of the acoustical ceiling tiles that I used for stages. I moved my "girls" around to the song, "A Pretty Girl Is Like a Melody," played on Grandmother's Victrola.

The store manager held a bolt of electric blue in front of me. "This is charmeuse, a popular new material. It's shiny like satin but not as heavy and gathers more easily."

I held the bolt under my chin.

"Yes, yes," he said, "a wonderful color for you."

I agreed. "Would you have feathers in the same color?"

"Marabou?" He opened a drawer and extracted a coil of blue fluff.

"Perfect," I said. "You think five yards of the feathers should be enough to go around the hem. I don't have time to make a second trip."

"Plenty, yes, plenty." He measured what I asked and coiled the feathers into a wreath.

Once upstairs, he cut several yards of the blue charmeuse, and tucked the folded fabric and the feathers into a plastic bag.

The total Mr. Middle East asked for was reasonable. Maybe a deal for a first-time customer with a reference.

Cradling the sack, I hot-footed back to my car—glad it was still there. Locked inside, I was determined not to get lost again, I gave full attention to my driving and soon found the southbound Harbor Freeway.

The next day after work I drove to Darla's. She measured me for both the bodice and the skirt.

"I need the dress weekend after next."

"I'll give your dress priority," she said. "Tomorrow, the bodice."

After work the next day, I was at the dressmaker's again. Agreeing that the bodice fitted well enough to proceed with the skirt, I left her shop with high hopes. Will this be a magic dress like Dorothy's sparkly red shoes? Will this happy blue transport me for a magical moment?

But the completed skirt was a shock. Darla had utilized the remaining material for the skirt—all nine yards. I hadn't realized I bought enough for a pup tent. *How am I to dance in something I can't even walk in?*

"This won't work," I told her. "I need the skirt to billow out as I turn around. It's too heavy. It clings."

"Clings?"

I spun around holding out my arms at shoulder height. "I want it to billow."

"Billow?"

Her eyes widened, her smile deepened. She nodded. "Come back in two days." And she helped me remove the dress.

Only five days left.

Two evenings later, I drove to her shop where in the tiny dressing room Darla helped me slip the costume over my head. She'd sewn a wire into the hem causing the skirt to bounce. *Shades of Gone with the Wind.* I stared at myself in the long mirror. I was encased in a hoop skirt only Scarlett could love.

I bowed to an invisible audience. *Oh, dear!* "Darla, I'm really sorry, but this hoop won't work."

"Why? Ma'am."

"When my partner holds me close, the skirt will tip up in back." *The audience will see more of me than I want. Maybe even which day of the week is embroidered on my fancy pants.*

The next time I entered Darla's shop, she met me with a sparkle in her dark brown eyes—and a petticoat of twenty-two rows of royal blue eyelet trim sewn on a cotton skirt of the same shade.

"This will be attached at the waist."

Sewing the three-layered skirt to the much lighter-weight bodice could not have been easy. I had to admire her skill. The skirt did billow, but to push the skirt ahead of me was like slogging through mud. *How can I do a high kick? Too late. I've run out of time.*

Darla surrounded the heavy garment with fresh white tissue and carefully packed it in one of her wedding boxes. With the cost of the dress, $350, the new shoes, $150, I guess I'd gotten off easy.

The morning of the Christmas benefit was clear and cool with an intense blue sky—the kind seen in commercials enticing people to California. I played Christmas music during the twenty miles I drove south on the 405.

Michael must have seen me park in front of the studio because he met me when I struggled to open the heavy glass door. "Here, let me help you." He took the garment bag containing the precious new dress and the recently dyed blue satin pumps. "Follow me," he said, moving up a long stairway to the airy second floor.

He pointed to a door halfway down the hallway to our right and knocked. A Lucy Ricardo look-alike peeked out. Seeing me, she opened the door wider, said, "I'll take that for her," and reached for the garment bag.

Michael called out, "When you're dressed, walk back down the hall to the main ballroom."

In the mirrored practice room-cum-dressing room were six mature women in various stages of undress. "Hi," I said, unfolding a chair and sitting down to remove my street shoes. Then, from its bag, I gingerly pulled out the heavy blue dress. This was the first time I'd put it on without Darla's help and the back zipper of the skirt eluded my grasp. My clammy hands couldn't even get a grip on the pull. I felt my face redden with the struggle. Help came in the form of the statuesque Lucy.

"Suck it in," she said, pointing at my stomach. Up went the side zipper and I felt the bodice contract like a corset. She gave my shoulder a pat. "One piece of advice. No matter what happens during your solo, keep smiling," and with that she sailed from the dressing room.

Once in their costumes, they all left for the ballroom.

I gathered my own be-feathered skirt, ready to take off like an aging blue swan, and followed the migration.

No! Your Other Left Foot

12

Disaster in Blue

I WALKED DOWN the dark passage kicking the heavy skirt before me. At the end I found a huge room with east and west facing windows. The afternoon sun flooded the space with light. Tables and chairs outlined the perimeter of a traditional polished wood floor. At the far end, on a small stage, stood a podium with a microphone.

Tall, blonde Patty, the advanced student who encouraged me to attend the Friday night parties, waved me over to our studio's reserved table in a corner. "Thea, that shade of blue is perfect for you, makes your eyes even bluer." She pinched my skirt. "Ooh. It's very soft and um, thick. How does it feel to walk in it?"

"Okay." Being a bit superstitious, I refrained from saying anything negative about the costume.

Couples in fancy dress glided onto the dance floor as a waltz blossomed from the speakers at the side of the stage. In an alcove under the east windows I saw tables covered with red and green Christmas paper displaying a variety of hors d'oeuvres and canapes, but I dared not risk spotting my dress.

Back in Massachusetts, where all houses had attics, my grammar school friends and I had delighted in playing dress-up with discarded clothes we found in old cartons and trunks.

Today, I was among a roomful of women in formals of all shades of the rainbow and men in suits and ties. A childhood fantasy come true. Trails of expensive perfume crisscrossed the room.

Michael stood at our table laughing with a friendly rival. Noticing me, he moved gracefully to my side. "That's a high energy color," he said. "I like it." He motioned for me to turn around.

I revolved slowly. Did the breeze created by the heavy skirt rustle Michael's spiky red hair?

"Whoa! That's a very full skirt. It's positively tubby."

"It's the best I could do without advice." I glared at him, but he didn't take the hint.

"Before we sit with the others, let's practice in the hall." He gently pushed me back down the hall. There we found another huge room with windows and mirrors everywhere. Ten couples danced in silence, apparently to tunes inside their own heads.

After leading me once through the routine, Michael said, "You're fine. Let's get back to our table."

The round tables held places for eight and six were already taken. Michael pulled out my chair and I lowered myself cautiously. Curious, he picked up a section of my skirt. He opened his mouth to comment, but the crackling of the PA system interrupted whatever he was going to say. The studio manager tapped the microphone. "Testing, one, two, three." He passed his professional smile around the room, then said,

No! Your Other Left Foot

"Ladies and gentlemen, please take your seats, and we'll begin our show."

The sound of shushing people whooshed around the room as conversations shut down.

"Welcome to our Fifth Annual Disadvantaged Children's Benefit. Today, you are all Mr. and Mrs. Claus, and, we promise you a dance treat as well." He glanced at the green paper program gripped in his hand. "First, dancing a waltz choreographed to Mannheim Steamroller's "Greensleeves" are Miss Thea Clark and her teacher, Michael Jensen."

I double-checked the program. Yes, our names in green ink in Old English font stared up at me. Suddenly I was gripped by terror. I reached for the cup of water.

"No more," Michael said. "You're just tense. You'll be fine. Now, we are going to walk over to that space between tables. Gather that crazy skirt, and smile."

His happy face swept the audience two tables deep on three sides of the floor.

Truly, he loves to perform.

"Stand straight, fan out your skirt. Pretend you're a butterfly." Leading me onto the smooth wooden surface, he whispered, "Here we go." He pulled me in his wake. In my free hand, I gathered my electric blue skirt with the feathered hem and swept the folds up and outward in a grand gesture.

Enthusiastic applause, topped by a whistle or two, greeted us as we toured the ballroom's perimeter. I saw the sea of grinning faces in slow motion. My heart thumped wildly.

Gently, Michael squeezed my hand and I turned to face him in closed dance position.

Whoops. There goes my stomach soaring toward my rattled brain. I reeled backward in time to another day of terror, when I'd stood at the stone altar of the Wayside Chapel overlooking Palos Verdes cliffs and the Pacific Ocean. I faced two men of the cloth, while my soon-to-be husband at my side cradled my lace-gloved hand in his. The polite clerical smiles of the ministers changed to broad grins as I opened my mouth to say, "I do." Unknown to me, the roll of Clorets breath mints I'd chewed on the curving drive around the hill had turned the inside of my mouth, lips and teeth a bright Kelly green.

I felt a tug on my arm. "Wake up, Thea!" said Michael, and we launched into the joyful waltz to the familiar melody of "Greensleeves."

The opening steps were perfection. We glided, we turned, we dipped. My tension eased as kinesthetic memory kicked in. Even dancing backwards in the unwieldy skirt didn't deter me, that is, until I caught the heel of my blue satin pump in a loop of thread where the marabou boa was sewn to the skirt's hem. For an interminable millisecond I became immobile, standing on one foot like a plump blue stork.

Michael felt my hesitation and tightened his grip on my back while I shook my shoe loose from the feathered hem.

"Remember," my glamorous red-headed friend had said earlier, "no matter what happens, keep smiling."

My quick rush of adrenaline as the flight-or-fight impulse surged apparently eluded the audience. Michael and I sailed on. But immediately another disaster loomed. Now, with both my feet on the floor, Michael led an inside turn and the cumbersome skirt belled outward. I was spun away, out of the security of his arms by the skirt's momentum. Without losing a beat, he caught up to me, whispering from the side of his mouth, "Thea, forget the routine. Follow whatever I do. Trust me."

My only recourse was to follow him. As if from far away, I heard Michael: "Remember, in a performance, you can't stop the music and ask to begin your routine over." He whispered fiercely, "And now for a big finish. Hang on! Pick up your skirt, hold it out, turn from me, then swing back into my arms."

Seconds later, we were bowing to applause.

"Hey. Congratulations." He laughed. "You hung in there, literally." His golden brown eyes shone. "I was surprised you reacted so quickly to my directions. I'm proud of you."

"I surprised myself. I'm proud of me, too."

At the close of the show, I packed Big Blue and accessories, waved goodbye to new friends and began the twenty-mile drive home, all the while singing Henry the Eighth's Christmas song.

It was time I let the whole family in on my new hobby.

13

Sixty-three Plus and Still My Mother's Child

MICHAEL'S FRIEND Don took Polaroids of the performers for his studio's scrapbook. He had captured the exact moment my heel caught in the hem. I wore a fixed smile, a wild look and a lot of Big Blue dress.

"Good shot!" Michael had exclaimed. He passed the picture to me. "Can Thea keep it?"

"Sure. I have others of you both, not as spectacular, but they'll do for the studio scrapbook."

I was grateful to Don for the photograph. At the next family lunch, I used it to introduce the subject of my secret avocation. "You all may have wondered about my new hobby."

The eleven faces around the dining room table waited expectantly. I passed around the photo.

"Wow!" said Luke. "Cool!" He winked at me. He always knew where I went, and I knew he wouldn't tell because his conversations with the family were limited. I was rewarded with looks of surprise and admiration. Then the questions came, and I spent a happy hour describing my lessons, the team match, and the Christmas Benefit.

Nana held the snapshot close to her eyes. "I didn't know you could do that." Then, she added wistfully, "When I was in my twenties, I loved to dance." She sighed. "Those dancing days ended when I married your father and moved to Panama. They had dances on the Base, but I was sick most of the time."

I was quiet, remembering the stories of how awful those five years had been for her.

"I wish I could see you dance," she said.

Caressing her hand lightly, I took the photo from her.

My year-long secret was out, I felt relief and regret.

Sadly, she never did see me dance. At ninety-four she could navigate her own bedroom, but she could not have seen me twenty feet away on the dance floor. No longer could she climb up and down our stairs without help. Most nights I brought up supper for the both of us, setting our places on TV tray tables. One evening in between mouthfuls, she said, "You've found your hobby at last. Now, what about a man?"

Two nights later, she asked, "Are you going out tonight?"

"Yes."

"For a lesson?"

"No. This is a Friday night party."

"Do you pay for it?"

"Yes."

"Well," she held out arms covered by a long-sleeved flannel nightie, "See? I'm all ready for bed."

"I'll be back in three hours."

"I won't wait up for you," she said. But I knew she'd try.

"Take your sweater," she called out as I left the room with our supper tray. "It looks cold outside."

Over sixty years old and still my mother's child.

14

$250 a Minute

Hey, you. You, with the West Point cadet posture. Where's that ol' couch potato of yore? I silently asked the hall mirror. Assuming an attitude, head and arms stretched upward, I let out a yell. Gone! Gone, by George.

The solo at Christmas had propelled me to a new level of confidence. But why hadn't I ended my amateur dancing career with this peak? Surely, it was time for me to let go of this expensive pastime.

But being the center of attention was fun. I mean, hells bells, I'd been the focus of 180 adolescents every day for thirty-five years at the local junior high, and yet at the end of my lesson plans, no one applauded.

These thoughts carried me into the studio for my weekly appointment where Michael sat at our usual table. "Well, Miss Thea, how do you feel now?"

I paused as I leaned over to pull out my dance shoes. *How do I feel? I feel happy to be here in a place I like with a person I like a lot. But how would I feel if I were no longer a part of this place?* "Sad," I replied, "really sad."

"Where were you, Thea?" Michael asked. "I've been talking to you about a competition."

"What? What competition?"

"In February of next year."

"Here?"

"No. In Vegas. Students and teachers from all over the United States and Canada will be there."

"I don't think so. Too big. Too scary."

"Look, Thea, you followed my directions perfectly. You carried on."

I got up and walked over to the bulletin board then read aloud, "Second Annual Challenge of Champions." I glanced back at Michael. "I thought this was for professional dancers."

"Truthfully, Thea, competitions couldn't survive without amateurs."

"Exactly what do you mean?"

"Money. Students fund both the studios and competition sponsors with their entry fees and what they spend at vendors' booths."

"Sort of like a golf tournament? The professionals compete for cash and the amateurs compete for fun. Sounds like big business to me."

"I'll bet you've never done anything like this before." His face lit up. "Weather is great in February. We could see a couple of shows, pretend to be eccentric millionaires. What do you say?"

"I don't know, Michael. I'm sure the whole thing is beyond my pocketbook." We sat not speaking, then I asked, "That's about five weeks from now, right?"

He nodded. "You'd need to give me an answer pretty soon. Entry fees are due two weeks before the comp begins."

How much do I want this? Where can I economize? "Will this competition be similar to the Team Match?"

"Yes and no. A lot more people participate. There are several judges for every heat, not just one as at the Team Match." He hesitated, reading my face. "Yes. Everything costs a lot more."

Oh, that grin with the dimples and fluttering eyelashes. Doing some quick mental calculations of lessons, travel and hotel costs, I said, "I could take a Caribbean cruise for the same amount, right?"

He was silent, barely breathing.

My eyes traveled around the studio. I noted the intent expressions of the couples on the floor. My ears reverberated with a samba beat. My heart ring-toned delight. *Just what is my happiness worth in dollars and cents?*

The following Friday night, during an intermission, Patty asked, "Are you going to Las Vegas with Michael?"

I hedged. "I don't know."

"Tom and I are going," she said.

"Tom is your son, right?"

She nodded and flashed a broad smile. "At eighteen, he's a very good dancer."

"Who's his partner?"

"His teacher, Christina Suarez."

"I'm curious. Why do you like to compete?"

"Gives me a goal for my regular lessons. Besides, I like to travel and renew friendships I've made through the competitions. I like the excitement and the glitz." Her hearty laugh underlined her statements. "And comps are a different lifestyle." She shrugged. "I have two lives. In teaching, my goal is to help my third graders do their best. In competing, the focus is on me, helps me bring out the best in me."

It might surprise her students' parents to see how glamorous this tall blonde really was.

I felt my pulse quicken. *Can I be glamorous too?* I was spurred to action. "Okay. I'll go. What do I do now?"

"Super!" Patty nodded and smiled. "Now," and she paused for effect, "you need a professionally-made ball gown."

Uh Oh. "Can't I use the blue dress?" I blushed, remembering the near fiasco. "With a few alterations?"

She wiped her face clean of laughter. "I'd retire that one. Use it for a costume at Halloween. That blue color was great for you but it was obvious the skirt was too bulky. I'd worry that it might bunch up between your legs and trip you."

She was too polite to say, "The only thing that would help that dress is a fire!" She continued, "When you dance a waltz, you want to appear light as a feather. You want to look elegant and feel beautiful. At least once in her life every woman needs to feel the magic of being Cinderella at her own ball."

Yes! Oh, to be the star of my own fairy tale!

Through my fantasy I heard Patty still talking. "I suggest

you talk to Lewis Suarez. He makes costumes for his wife and some of his students. He'll give you good advice."

I pondered the cost of that three-minute Christmas solo, the unusable dress and the ill-fitting pumps I'd probably never wear again because I bought the wrong size. Add the benefit's expense, and my total for everything was roughly $750.

Blimey! My solo cost a hefty $250 per minute, which put it in the lawyer, doctor, Golden Door category. Am I worth $250 per minute?

You betcha.

15

What's a Body Suit?

MICHAEL'S GROUP CLASSES were the only sessions I'd ever attended. He was my comfort zone. However, I took Patty's advice and the next Friday night joined Mr. Suarez's East coast swing.

Twice the width of Michael and an inch taller, Lewis Suarez had thick, straight, inky black hair and onyx eyes that became luminous when he laughed. His stature was commanding; he looked more like a young Placido Domingo than a dancer.

Gesturing toward the women in the group, he said, "Welcome to East coast swing. Ladies, line up facing me." He noticed me, nodded, and smiled.

"Men, form a line alongside me." After reviewing the basic steps he'd taught the group the previous week, he asked, "Any questions?" People shook their heads.

I kept mum. I knew only two of the four steps he'd demonstrated, but I was too shy to ask for a repeat.

"First, I'll show the men how to lead the women, then I'll show the women their part." He danced with every woman in turn. Following that, Mr. Suarez said, "Partner up while I put on the music."

We were one man short and he filled in, changing partners after four or five steps so every woman experienced the correct lead. When he came to me, I did my best to follow and talk at the same time. "May I speak to you about a costume?" I asked.

"Sure," he said. "After class, okay?" Then he went on to the next woman on my right. She was petite, probably a disgusting size zero. I couldn't figure out how he led her without bending over double to accommodate their height difference.

Could the man have a hydraulic backbone?

"That was great, Marge," he said to her, gently squeezing her shoulder before moving on.

At the close of class, the group drifted to tables seating four, arranged along the street side of the studio, chatting while waiting for the practice party to begin.

Mr. Suarez approached my table. I glanced up at him as he pulled out a chair.

"Patty," I said, "you know Patty?"

He nodded.

"She suggested I talk to you about a ball gown."

"Do you have something particular in mind?"

"I already have a dress I wore at the Christmas Benefit, but she says it's not right for the competition in Las Vegas."

"You're going with Michael?"

"Yes." I was surprised that he knew. I guess dance teachers talk about their students just as public school teachers do.

"I'm taking students also," he said.

"Oh, great." I grinned then returned to my point. "Patty

says the blue gown I wore at the Benefit is too unwieldy for competition."

"Possibly." He appeared thoughtful. "Are you staying for tonight's dance?"

"Uh, huh."

"Good. We can talk before the dance starts. Just a sec. I'll get some sketch paper. And," he smiled, "please call me Lewis."

"Okay, Lewis. I saw you dance with your wife at the Benefit, but since I'm not your student, you probably didn't notice me."

"Not exactly easy to miss you," he said with a chuckle. "You were first on the program. The color of your dress made your eyes bluer. But what made the skirt so…so *big*?"

I told him about the many incarnations of Big Blue, including the Scarlet O'Hara hoop.

He laughed. "Non-dancers don't always understand how dance costumes are constructed. The difference is the body suit."

"The what?"

"Let me show you." He sketched a strapless bathing suit. "This body suit is usually made of the same color material as the bodice. It's like a foundation or an undergarment. The skirt is attached to that later. He sketched as he talked. "Do you remember the one-piece bathing suits popular in the nineteen fifties? He looked a little sheepish as though he might have said something offensive.

"Of course. I wore one. But you weren't there, you're too

young. I imagine you're somewhere in your twenties?"

"Somewhere." He winked. "Anyway, that's when Spandex was first used. You need to have an undergarment that gives when you perform developes.

"Oh, I know about developes. High kicks, you mean?"

"Like when you caught your heel?"

I winced. "I thought we covered that up."

"Another dancer, especially a teacher, would notice. So, tell me what you want in a ball gown."

"I'd like long sleeves to cover my flabby upper arms. And I would like to appear thinner if possible."

"I can do that. Anything else?"

"Yes. I'd like to be several inches taller and a better dancer."

His laugh came from deep in his barrel chest. "I can only do so much."

His simple sketch showed a front and back version of a calf-length dress with a modest neckline, long sleeves, a waistline dipping to a point and . . .

"There's no back!" I squeaked.

"Most competition costumes show a lot of the woman's back."

"Oh, all right. What are these scratches around the hem?"

"Ostrich feathers. Feathers are popular because they add excitement and movement."

"How long would it take you to make such a dress?"

"If you're serious, we need to buy the fabrics tomorrow or

the next day."

"Okay, about how much would such a dress cost?"

Without skipping a beat—after all, he was dancer—he said, "In the two thousand dollar neighborhood."

Oh. Back to that neighborhood.

No trips next year either.

I focused on his line drawing. "What fabrics are we talking about?"

"Satin is good because of its lustrous sheen and it ripples like water. Do you know what I mean?"

I took a deep breath. *I can mortgage my condo maybe.* Did Lewis have a magical touch of Glenda the Good Witch of the West to create a Cinderella dress for me?

I'd soon find out.

I met Lewis at the local fabric store where my mother shopped for most of the clothes in my closet. She knew it well. After all, she'd made my clothes till I was fifty!

We drove into the large parking lot in tandem although we'd come from different areas of the city. I smiled when I saw his high five. That gesture warmed me and I parked my car with a happy heart.

"Let's go right to the satin section," he said, marching off on a mission. "First, you must be sold on the color." Pointing toward a nearby table, he removed bolts in quick succession and held lengths of luscious hues under my chin from shoulder to shoulder: red, turquoise, green, blue, and lavender.

No color sang to us until he held under my chin a bolt of a mouth-watering peach.

"Yes!" we said in unison.

Lewis rewound the bolt, tucked it under his arm and headed to the service counter where he told the clerk the number of yards he wanted. I winced, remembering the extra unnecessary yards I'd purchased for Big Blue.

Next, he strode purposefully toward the Spandex section. Selecting a shade to match the peach, he took that bolt to the clerk. "Two yards, please." He turned to me. "For the body suit." And now, let's find the lace for the top."

The clerk tipped her head toward stairs at the end of the huge room. Quickly, Lewis climbed them, checking over his shoulder to make sure I followed.

Displayed on the second floor were row upon row of fragile fabrics in rainbow hues. He knew what he wanted and pointed to a delicate pink lace. "This will do."

I protested. "Pink with peach. It's not an exact match."

Trust me," he said. "This combination will work."

Trust you? I barely know you! We're talking major dollars here.

Back on the first floor, he handed the bolt of lace to the cashier. Turning to me, he said, "I need to take some measurements so I can begin the bodysuit. Okay if I do that here?"

"At the cashier's counter?" I shrugged. "Sure."

Unwinding the tape wrapped around his planner he began at my bust. I didn't know I had so many measurements:

center front to waist, back waist to knee, waist, hip rise, girth, sleeve length, bust, over-bust, ribcage to waist, and waist to calf.

The data recorded, he collected the packages of fabric amounting to a little under seventy-five dollars. On the way to our cars he said, "The skirt will have pleats graduating from narrow at the waist to wide at the hem."

"Wow! That's a lot of work." *Do I get charged by the pleat?*

"Oh, the pleats will be mechanically pressed. Not to worry, they'll be evenly spaced."

A few days later he arrived at my townhouse carrying a small sewing machine and a Nordstrom's suit box. From the latter, he removed the peach-colored Spandex body suit. He had instructed me earlier to wear only a bra and panty hose. When the doorbell rang, I opened the door dressed as he requested, a short Japanese kimono over my bra and undies. I'd only met him fully clothed twice, and already we were on underwear footing. *Hey, I'm a senior citizen and only so many more years to be adventurous. I can cope with this.*

"Today," he said. "I need to adjust the suit for a tight fit, but please be careful handling it. The side seams are only basted. Hold the fabric gently as you step into the leg holes."

Moving through the living room to the dining room, I said, "The light's best in here. You can put your machine on the glass dining room table."

Sunlight through the windows was generous at that time

of the afternoon. The satin caught the light and reflected ripples of peach liquid as Lewis gently lifted the bathing suit–like article from its resting place. Handing it to me, he warned again, "The side seams are only basted."

I carried the yard of slippery cloth through the living room into the nearby bathroom and closed the door. Tossing my kimono aside, I gingerly pulled on the satin outfit. That is, I tugged, twisted, pulled, and panted.

"Everything all right in there?" Lewis had approached the other side of the bathroom door. "Do you need help?"

I'm tugging; I'm aware he's listening. Finally, I said, "It's really tight . . . ."

"Supposed to be close-fitting," he called. "Where is it too tight, exactly?"

"The crotch." *I'm so old, I can remember having to stay after school for saying that word in ninth grade history class.*

Then, I remembered a college incident and chuckled. In 1950 I wore the Playtex rubber girdle with the built-in crotch. All the girls I knew had one even though they were expensive—from nine to eleven dollars each. Girls like me in the plus sizes felt the cost was well worth it. The rubber casing flattened the tummy and solidified the buttocks like two giant hands squashing the wayward flesh together. The girdle came inside a cardboard tube with directions to help you get the darn thing on. The rubber waistband eventually stretched with constant pulling, and in the powder rooms of that era, when you heard "Oh, my God!" everyone knew just what had just happened. Someone's girdle had split down the back, slithered to the floor, silk stockings still attached to the now useless garters. No safety pins, Scotch tape, nor needle and thread could put those babies back together again.

The college set referred to the garment as the WWII chastity belt. I recalled a maudlin first date with a USC freshman. After an evening of dancing to the Harry James band at the Hollywood Palladium, he drove me back to my dorm in Westwood. I'd not been particularly taken with him, and when he became amorous, I purposely snapped my rubber waist band.

"Damn!" he said as he returned to the driver's side of his father's Dodge. "Are you wearing one of those vulcanized discouragers? I might as well walk you to your door right now."

Lewis's worried voice brought me back to the present. "Otherwise does it fit okay?"

"I can't raise my arms and I don't think I can sit down."

"Can you come out and show me? The suit needs to be tight so that you'll keep your frame."

Removing the suit took almost as long as putting it on. Finally, I held the delicate garment through a crack in the door.

I sat on the toilet waiting for Lewis to tell me what to do next.

"I've pulled out some of the basting. Please, try it on one more time. Carefully!"

This time, I managed to work the bodysuit on with fewer gyrations and less cursing. Opening the bathroom door, I stood still for his inspection.

"Good," he said, turning me around. "After I machine-stitch the seams, we'll do one last try-on today, then I'll take it with me to attach the skirt."

He returned the next day. The sleeves had been connected to the bodice, the bodice connected to the skirt and the skirt connected to the bodysuit.

Now hear the words of the Lord. Hummm.

"Next step, the stoning," he said.

"Stoned? Are we talking drugs here?"

He laughed. "No. No."

"Explain to me 'stoning'."

"I'll glue hundreds of rhinestones on the lace bodice and the sleeves, one at a time. I use Austrian crystal, they're the most brilliant. When the intense spotlights in the ballroom strike the stones, there is an explosion of light as the dancer moves."

"Is everything in competing an illusion?" I asked.

"Not quite," he said. "You still have to dance well to score high."

Before he left, I handed Lewis a five hundred dollar check for the crystals.

A quick tally of escalating costs weakened my knees. I could re-carpet my apartment for the price of the dress, but, dammit, new rugs weren't nearly as exciting as prancing in a Cinderella gown.

When I told Lewis I was curious about how he applied the rhinestones, he said, "Here, I'll put some in this scrap of lace and you can practice. Do you have a glue gun?"

Immediately, I appreciated his skill. To my disgust, I burned one finger on the glue gun and adhered stones to my thumb. Clicking my fingers and thumb together did not a flamenco dancer make.

A couple of days later a knock on the door signaled his presence. Smiling, he held out the white suit box as though it were a special prize. "Hi. Ready for a try-on?"

"Yes." I returned the smile.

Lewis placed the familiar box on the couch, and when he pulled out the finished dress I gasped.

I can't believe this beautiful creation is just for me. "I love it, Lewis!"

He nodded happily. "I'm glad. Do you need help putting it on?"

"Probably with the hook at the back and the zipper." I quickly walked to the bathroom, excitedly carrying the dress in both arms. Moments later I emerged in my new peach satin, diamond-studded gown with feathers dripping from each sleeve and encircling the hem. Even my wedding gown hadn't been this elaborate.

"Turn around so I can zip you up," said Lewis. After he'd locked the zipper in place, he smoothed the fabric on my shoulders, then he pulled the waist down front and back, shaking out the skirt. Satisfied, he said, "Now, whirl so I can see the full effect."

I whirled.

"Yes," he continued, "this dress will work for you. Remember, you are the star, the dress is only to enhance your dancing." Then he changed the subject. "I'll call Michael and have him meet us at the studio." He flipped his appointment book. "Saturday, okay? I need to see the two of you dancing so I can take action photos for my scrapbook."

I was childlike in my anticipation the morning of the "dress" rehearsal. Through the studio's corner window, Michael and Lewis saw my arrival in the parking lot. Opening the studio door Lewis said, "Here, I'll take your garment bag and hang it up in the dressing room." He took the precious cargo as Michael gave me a hello hug.

"Are you excited, Miss Thea?" Michael asked.

I giggled, shuddered and nodded. Words weren't there; tears of happiness trembled on the brink.

Inside the small room, not much more than a storage closet, I closed the door, unzipped the bag, removed the dress and laid it over a folding chair. I stared at the most beautiful dress I'd ever owned. I wanted to cherish the moment. *Don't waste the guys' time. Get dressed.*

I set aside sheets of white tissue from my shopping bag, then spread them on the not-so-clean floor. The pink feathers around the skirt's hem were pristine and I wanted them to stay that way. Christina, Lewis's wife, had dyed my brand new satin pumps the same soft peach of the gown.

I checked the lock on the door, then removed all my street clothes. Hopping on one leg at a time, I stepped into the body suit. In order to pull the tight-fitting garment on and at the same time push my arms through the sleeves, I had to gather all the layers of skirt material and roll them into folds, clutching the fat bunch to my waist. The yards of satin and taffeta were slippery, and I worried about crushing the pleats. Finally, I was inside the garment.

With my arms stretched around my back, I grasped the zipper and crawled it upward until I reached the hook and eye.

I'm in, but can I breathe? So far I hadn't popped off any of those expensive Swarovski crystals nor molted any feathers. I sighed in relief.

Thea, take little sips of air until you can breath normally. Viewing myself in the long mirror on the back of the door, I turned to the right then the left. I glowed. I sparkled. I looked terrific. Happiness poured over me like warm maple syrup.

Savor this moment, Thea. The thousands you've spent have led up to this. Uh oh. Something was missing. Oops! I'd forgotten the pretty pumps, so newly changed from their white satin that I could still smell a whiff of dye.

Could I bend over? Perhaps if I lined up the shoes at the back of the chair and held on to the metal rim, and if I was really slow and careful, I could step into them. Again I gathered the slippery skirt, bunching it loosely at the waist so I could see the shoes while I pushed my feet, one at a time into their tight and shiny interiors. Removing a wayward feather from my mouth, I breathed deeply and opened the door to the ballroom.

The two men shared an ice cream parlor table, the small table top holding Lewis's sewing machine, and a video camera. They stood in unison, smiled and applauded. We approached each other in slow motion, meeting in the center of the floor.

"Miss Thea, you look splendid." Michael winked. "I swear, if you were thirty years younger ..."

Lewis, nodded in agreement. "Michael, waltz her around the floor while I videotape."

Michael held out his arms, the signal for me to step forward into dance position, and then he moved me gently into a basic waltz step.

Oh, this is fine—really fine. This skirt is feather-light. It goes exactly where I want it to go.

We waltzed the perimeter of the floor twice, then Lewis called out, "Michael, have Thea stand still and spread the skirt like butterfly wings."

He aimed his camera. "Now, Thea, turn slowly. Hold your skirt as high as you can as if you were getting ready to fly. Remember Audrey Hepburn descending those long stairs in *Funny Face?* Like that."

"Like this, Lewis?"

"Yes. Great."

No! Your Other Left Foot

I twirled happily. *What a wonderful feeling! I don't want the morning to end.*

"Thank you. That's fine, Thea."

I dropped my wings and stood still for a moment.

Oohh. I'm all dressed up with nowhere to go.

Michael sat to remove his dance shoes; Lewis packed his camera and sewing kit.

"Anything else?" I asked, hoping there would be. I wasn't quite ready to discard my butterfly persona. I vaguely remembered a poem but not the name of the poet:

Three caterpillars responded differently
To a butterfly that happened by:
The first said, "Just look at that fellow giving himself airs!"
The second said, "How I'd love to fly like that."
The third said, "Why, that's me!"

16

Nana and Luke

AGLOW WITH ANTICIPATION for the adventure in Las Vegas, I sat at my bedroom desk listing items to pack. First, I called Stacy at the beauty parlor. "I'm going to Las Vegas in February."

"What fun," said Stacy.

"I'm not going to gamble, but to compete."

"Compete in what?" she asked.

"Ballroom dancing."

"Oh," she said. "I have a client who is a champion, Kathryn Shaeffer. Do you know her?"

"I don't know any professionals except my teacher. It's my first competition and I need a new look." We set an appointment for the end of the week.

That night, as I fantasized how I'd appear in short hair and a long gown, I heard Nana's trembly call for help from her bedroom across the hall. Half off the toilet, she was slumped toward the bathroom floor. I rushed forward to prop her up. Piling cushions around her, I left to phone. *Thank God for 911.*

The paramedics sped her to San Pedro Peninsula Hospital two miles away. Diagnosed as having had a medium stroke, she remained for several days under observation then she was moved to the hospital's rehabilitation unit for three weeks before she was allowed to come home.

My job and dancing were now secondary to Nana's welfare. I spent hours first at the hospital, then at the rehab center, grateful that Nana was so strong and motivated to recover. Comfortable once again in her own room, Nana worked with a physical therapist three times a week to recover mobility.

"You do better leg lifts than I do." I told her. "I'm impressed."

"Just following doctor's orders," she muttered.

I couldn't believe how this ninety-four year old was so motivated to regain her independence. Every day, I watched her leg crossovers and mini-sit-ups as she faithfully followed the prescribed exercises. One morning, I approached a touchy subject. "Your therapist suggested a walker. When she comes tomorrow, she'll show you the proper way to use one."

"Don't want a walker. Won't use."

"Nana, you need it for balance and support."

"It'll just clutter up my bedroom."

Knowing further discussion would be useless, I sighed and switched topics. Nevertheless, I bought the walker the therapist suggested.

Sadly, my mother's window of independence slowly and inevitably closed. She fought to hold on to activities she could do without my help, but I worried that she'd go beyond her capabilities—for instance, going downstairs alone.

I remembered the toddler's gate gathering dust in the garage, the restraint we'd used when Luke was little. But locking that across the stairs would really tick her off. She'd probably try to undo it, resulting in both of them collapsing.

"Please, Nana, wait until I return from work to go downstairs. Please!"

She gave me a stony look.

I continued, "In case I can't get home at lunchtime, I've fixed a sandwich, a small salad, and a pudding. "I'll leave everything on a tray in your room."

Truly, I was terrified I'd find her sprawled unattended for hours. Should I quit work? Some years ago, late one afternoon, she'd missed the front porch step—or had a transitory stroke, we never knew which—and lay helpless on the cement walkway until I got home from work. That memory still haunted me. I contemplated my options: quit my job to take care of her full time, or bring in a caregiver. I'd hate the former; she'd fight the latter. I did buy a portable potty to keep by her hospital bed. When she saw it, she said, "Now you don't have to get up to help me use the toilet."

"We'll see," I murmured.

"If you'd leave one bedrail down I can swing my legs over and get out of bed by myself." She added, "You need your sleep. Why did you go back to work anyway? We don't need the money."

Here we go again with the guilt trip. I didn't bother to argue. Besides, now we did need the money.

Suddenly, Nana had a bad night. I still shiver when I recall the scene. Around four a.m., I heard a little girl's voice whispering for help. I leapt out of bed and rushed across the hall. I couldn't believe what I saw. I found her with her legs wrapped around the bed railing as though she'd been climbing a horizontal rope in her sleep. I stood looking at her. *How in hell am I going to unwind her?*

I screamed for fifteen-year-old Luke. It was a desperate long shot. His bedroom was at the other end of the hall, where after blasting his heavy metal sounds behind a closed door, he slept soundly. Miraculously, he appeared at my side.

"Dude!" he said softly. Then, in a soothing voice directly into her ear, he said, "Nana. Luke here. I'm going to help you. You'll be all right. Let go of the rail one arm at a time. Grab my shoulder." He bent over her and touched her icy hand.

She shook her head, her eyes wide with terror.

He took one of her hands, gently prying open stiffened fingers. "That's good. Now put your hand on my arm and squeeze."

She glared at him, but did as she was told, grabbing his shoulder as quick as a frog catches a fly.

"That's good. Now, the other arm." He grunted as he shifted her upper body from the railing over onto him.

"Good. Now, relax your legs."

Her arms locked around his neck, her thighs still cemented to the metal.

"Nana, let go of the railing. I have you."

She squeezed her eyes shut, tears dribbling down her cheeks. Finally she released her legs. Enclosing her whole limp body in his arms, Luke began issuing orders. "Grandma, pull the blankets away from her legs." He took a deep breath, "Quick! Grandma, straighten the bedclothes."

That done, he lowered her gently and pulled the covers over her flaccid arms. Giving her sparse gray hair a pat, he said, "Good night, Nana. Sleep tight!" Then all six feet of him loped back to his own room.

Luke, our family's troubled teenager, had lived with Nana and me for a year. He disliked school and was often suspended for fighting. "Never performs to his potential," his report cards stated.

In this emergency, he proved them wrong.

My job with Oasis was a welcome distraction from the tensions at home. One day Nana said, "I thought you were semi-retired." Pausing for effect, she continued, "You only go to your office to get away from me."

True. But then if I don't work, I have no uninterrupted private time—and more importantly, I can't afford dance lessons. Only to myself did I admit that I was increasingly resentful of my mother's dependence on me.

Las Vegas was beckoning. What to do?

My two grown children supported my plan to hire a caregiver. One evening as Nana and I shared a light supper, I said, "A woman named Maria will be here while I'm at work. She was referred to me by a friend who says she's a good worker, quiet and trustworthy."

Nana pouted and her blue eyes darkened.

"We have to do this, Nana. I'm not going to quit my job. I like my work. I like the extra money."

She fumed and spit out her resentment. "I don't know why you can't stay home."

I held up my hand for silence. "I'm firm on this, Nana."

The next morning I brought in Maria and left the room to let them get acquainted. She was shorter than my mother, plump and tidy. Peeking through the partially-closed door, I listened to the conditions Nana spelled out, saw Maria nod and smile.

Only because Maria was attentive and patient did we survive that first week. She bathed Nana, helped her dress, and carried upstairs the meals I'd made before I left for work.

Often when I got home, I'd see Maria sitting on a hassock at Nana's right, crocheting the children's blankets she eventually sent home to Mexico. Soon Nana was regaling her with stories of her own New England past and childhood.

"Maria appreciates me more than you do," Nana announced one evening. "Maria loves me."

Hallelujah, thank you, Jesus.

The next day, daughter Karen said, "Go to Las Vegas, Mom. Have fun. Maria and I can take care of Nana."

17

Las Vegas

Six weeks after the December children's benefit and the waltz solo in Big Blue, Michael and I met at the Los Angeles International Airport. With a dozen teachers and students from the dance studio, we headed for Las Vegas. Over my arm hung the new garment bag containing my precious ball gown. For a moment, I'd considered buying the dress its own seat. Or, maybe giving it my seat and checking myself in with the pets.

"Let me help you with your bags," Michael said as he came up the escalator behind me. Unexpectedly, tiny bubbles of perspiration bloomed on Michael's face, something that rarely happened at the studio.

"Are you feeling okay?"

He gave me a tight smile.

Later, strapped in, I glanced at Michael when he dabbed at his forehead. "Flying makes me nervous," he said, "especially the take-off. I'll be all right once we're in the air."

I winced, recalling the previous day's conversation after practice. I'd been changing shoes when he asked if I had a moment to talk. Straightening, I gave him my full attention. "Is this about flying?"

"Ah, no. There's a situation developing I can't talk much

about." He paused as if waiting for me to say something.

"I don't know what you mean," I said.

"Have you paid the whole fee for the competition?"

"Yes, of course. The manager asked for a check last week."

He murmured, "Well, that's that. It's probably been deposited already."

"What's this really about, Michael?" At once, I felt wary; the air around me grew heavy. While I waited for the explanation, I took several quick breaths. My stomach fluttered. I gulped water from my sports bottle.

He bowed his head. I could barely hear him. "Since you paid the whole three thousand, I won't back out."

I went rigid. "You won't what?" I felt I'd screamed that question, but then realized I'd barely whispered. "Are you saying you can't dance?"

"It's not that I don't want to dance." He cleared his throat. "Honestly, I want to go. You just need to know ahead of time there may be problems."

"Michael, just what would keep us from competing?" *Health troubles? I hope not.*

"I can't talk about the details now. Trust me. I want to. Truly, I do. In fact, I've already invited some friends in Vegas to come watch us."

This was news to me. "When were you planning to tell me about all this?" My fantasies of wowing my friends and family with my first and perhaps my only triumphant performance in Las Vegas were fast disappearing. The money expenditure alone fired my anger. I'm sure my feelings were reflected on my face.

"I do want to go," he repeated in a little boy's voice, piercing my emotional fog. "I truly want to dance with you."

"Then I'm making the decision for both of us. We'll get on the plane. We'll deal with whatever happens day by day."

And now, we were side by side and airborne. I looked down at his hands white knuckling the seat's metal arms, leaving perspiration silhouettes. Once in the air Michael relaxed and closed his eyes for the rest of the flight.

Squinting through the Plexiglass at the receding landscape, I focused on the face there. My reflection revealed my mouth moving in silent prayer. *I refuse to spoil these next four days and nights with negative imaginings.*

My costumes totaled two thousand five hundred and fifty-five dollars. Airfare, hotel, and entrance fees were all included in a package costing three thousand. This little adventure ended up costing a thousand dollars a day. I was sure as heck going to get my money's worth.

The hour flight seemed longer, the minutes filled with "what ifs" moving like a ticker tape across the conscious part of my mind. I scolded myself. *I intend to be alert and aware every moment.*

Patty and her seventeen-year-old son, Thomas, sat behind us. Because she and I both taught for LA Unified School District, we shared experiences. But not body types, shapes, nor height. She was almost as tall as her six-foot son. Her short blonde hair haloed a peach bloom complexion and a sparkling smile.

When at last the plane touched the tarmac and Michael was able to feel terra firma, I saw his shoulders straighten, and a grin once more spread across his lean face. "Here, let me carry the garment bag for you."

In the hotel lobby, we joined the hundreds of people who milled, chatted, laughed and complained. Gamblers and dancers, seniors and athletes in designer jeans and shorts, all mingled trying to appear patient.

Back home, Patty and I had decided to ease the escalating expenses by sharing a room four ways: her friend, Linda, Patty's son, and me. Michael would bunk in with the other teachers. With every step closer to the reception desk, I sensed Michael's tension. He kept shifting his feet, vibrating the air between us.

"What's wrong?" I asked.

He glanced behind us to see where the manager stood then whispered, "The studio suspects I'm sick. I've heard there's to be a meeting about me when we get back to L.A. I'll probably be fired, but before that, I'll quit." He patted an inner pocket. "I have my letter of resignation with me just in case."

Damnation. Anger and frustration boiled up within me. I was angry at him for being unwilling to do all I thought he should do to be healthy. Other times I was mad at God for this devastating disease.

I took stock of the current situation: four people ahead of

us in line. In a split second I made a radical decision. I touched Michael's arm gently. "I'm going to get a private room. We can share that and you won't have to be with the manager and other teachers."

He frowned. "That's extra expense for you."

I ram-rodded my posture. "Priorities, Michael. If you can't dance well, I won't look good either."

Our turn came at the desk. I plunked down my credit card, requesting a room change. You'd thought I had a gas explosion by the expression on the clerk's face.

"But you are sharing a room with a Mrs..." she squinted at her computer "...Ertzman."

"I've changed my mind."

I could see her lips forming the words "You can't do that," but the set-in-stone look on my face and the impatience of the others in the long line behind me precluded argument. She hit the keys on the keyboard as though she were spanking a wayward child. "You're very fortunate. We've just had a vacancy on the floor with your other companions."

A bellboy followed us with our luggage to the elevator. When I saw Patty at the back I said, "I've made a change. I'll call you."

Once inside with our luggage unloaded, I asked Michael, "Which bed do you want?"

"Doesn't matter. Which side of the closet would you like?"

"Doesn't matter," I said.

I was unpacking when the phone rang. Michael looked at me for permission. "Go ahead," I said.

I heard the studio manager's voice loud and very clear. In no uncertain terms he yelled that Michael had better get his butt and bags to the teachers' suite immediately. "Teachers aren't allowed to fraternize with students, especially not . . ." He left the remains of the sentence hanging in the air.

"I'm sorry, Thea. Perhaps this is best after all." He repacked, then closed the door quietly behind him.

Now, I had a room to myself at twice the cost I'd originally planned on. *The price per hour for this hobby has just gone up—again.* Actually, I felt relieved. I'd seen Michael chain smoke at parties; I was an intolerant ex-smoker. And, I'd just as soon not have my costumes smell of smoke.

18

Glitz, Glitter, Glamour

THE COMPETITION OFFICIALLY began that evening with a formal banquet open to the public.

"This is more like the elegance I was expecting," I said to Patty when I arrived at our reserved table.

Sparkling silver decorations hung in swags from the huge mirrored ball in the ceiling's center. Fresh floral centerpieces decorated the dozens of round tables arranged on three sides of the highly polished wood dance floor. Along the fourth wall at a raised dais sat the tournament officials, all in formal attire.

Michael wore his best suit—not his competition tails—but a heathery tweed which added a few pounds to his thin frame. He stood chatting with two other men, also in business suits near our reserved table. He smiled, mouthing *come join us*. Taking my hand, he said, "Great dress." Then, "This is my student, Miss Thea."

I didn't know whether to bow or just smile.

"She's competing against your ladies tonight, Steve." To me he said, "Steve and I knew each other in Florida."

The other men waved goodbye and in tandem said, "Break a leg."

By this time, we'd reached our reserved table. I pointed to the white orchid corsage attached to my place card. "This for me?"

Michael nodded. He extended his hand as though inviting me to dance. I automatically placed my hand in his. "Let me slip this on your wrist. Perfect." And he held out my chair while I gathered my many-layered black chiffon skirt.

I smiled at the elderly couple seated across from me. The man spoke. "We love coming to these competitions. Actually, we prefer the professional dance performances to the girlie shows." He touched the hand of his white-haired companion clothed in a royal blue formal. "Here, we can dance together between the heats." He gave his partner a sweet smile. She patted his hand.

I thought of my mother. She longed to dance with my father. Now, she was less and less able to see the TV and couldn't distinguish me from any other people at the dance studio, even if she'd been brought there on a Friday night. I'll be at a crossroads soon. What can I decide about her future?

My watch said seven o'clock, an hour and a half to go before my first heat. Torn between wanting to collect glorious details to take back home and the need to focus on my own upcoming performance, I failed to answer a question from the gentleman at our table. "I'm sorry," I said, "I can't seem to concentrate on the conversation." I turned to Michael. "I need to change into my costume. I'll be back in plenty of time for the Newcomers heats."

"Are you all right?"

"I'm nervous, that's all."

Patty asked, "Need any help with your dress?"

"Probably. I still find it hard to hook the back once I get the zipper up."

"Just call my room if you need me," she said. "I'm skipping dessert."

Michael stood to pull out my chair. "Wait, I'll go up with you. I need to iron my tails. You can call me too, if you want."

He really is a sweet person. I won't think about his health problems.

Once in my own room, changing into my peach dress wasn't a problem until I came to that dreaded zipper. My shaking fingers just couldn't manage it. *I'll call Patty after I put on my makeup.*

Fifteen minutes later and there she was at the door complete in her own vermillion chiffon be-feathered finery. "Okay, how can I help?"

I turned my back to her. She zipped me up and fastened the top hook. The bodice fit tight like a corset. She patted my shoulders and tugged down the lower part of the bodice smoothing out any wrinkles. "Check yourself in the mirror. You're all set to go. Your makeup looks good too. Could use a dash more blush." She hunted for the rouge and, picking up the brush, added another layer highlighting my cheekbones. "The intense spotlights wash out color, you have to exaggerate your makeup."

"Thank you. I really appreciate your help. And good luck to you tonight, too."

She waved at the door and swept out and on down the hall.

I donned the black velvet opera cape my best friend had loaned me. The soft plushness comforted me. I felt queenly and elegant. Locking my room, I too swished down the hallway to the elevator and down the seventeen floors to the casinos. I floated past the steadfast gamblers and bashfully returned their smiles.

This is going to be a wonderful night. Closer and closer to the ballroom, I strode straighter and taller. *I will make this adventure memorable.*

I traveled fully armed with my dance bag of essentials: my room key, my extra shoes, tissues, makeup, plus a small bag of trail mix should I happen to get lost in the Las Vegas wilderness.

Peeking inside the ballroom, I saw that the remains of the grand banquet had been cleared away except for the glittering decorations and, of course, the traditional mirrored ball. After showing my ticket to the two security men at the double doors, I sought Michael.

There he stood, halfway down the left side of the huge room talking with two other teachers also in the uniform of the day: white ties and tails. Shades of Robert Taylor in Camille, or Cary Grant trailing Katherine Hepburn covering her exposed behind. I love the look of men in formal dress, shooting their cuffs, straightening their ties—so Edwardian. So Jane Austen.

Michael had let his hair return to its natural curly light

brown; no red spikes for the competition. His chiseled features emphasized his austere elegance but the dark smudges under his eyes bothered me.

"Am I too early?" I asked. "Where are all the people who come to watch?" I waved a hand at the bleachers.

"Mostly family and friends come to watch Newcomers and Beginners. When the more advanced level heats begin, seats will fill up," He glanced me up and down. "You look very nice. Are you ready to dance?"

I shrugged. "I have no idea what happens next."

"Find us in your program. Mark the pages where our names appear. Circle our entry number. We line up chronologically. Be prepared to keep track. The heats move fast. They will call your name once, maybe twice. If you are not in the lineup, you forfeit." He pointed at a gap in the tables. "See that empty space near the front door? That's where we are to be for roll call. Hey, there's Patty. I bet she came to root for you."

"Hurray," I said softly and mouthed a "thank you."

We gave each other the A-frame hug to avoid accidentally hooking our bodices on each other's sequins and stones.

The electricity in the atmosphere crackled. "It's time," said Michael, indicating with his chin. "That woman holding a clipboard over there. She's checking in the competitors."

"Don't we rehearse or anything?"

He nodded and pointed to a space in the corner of the room, clear of tables and people.

"It's carpeted there. My shoes will stick."

"Don't worry about that. We need to get used to holding each other."

Suddenly, I was shy. My first lessons had been at arm's length. One day, he said, "Now, you're ready for closed dance position." I wasn't sure what he meant until he held me just a few inches from his own body, my left hip touching his right. *Talk about electricity.*

"Let's do some waltz steps."

I stumbled. He caught me. "You're just nervous. You'll do fine. On to the lineup." He held onto my left hand tightly. I wondered if he were praying as hard as I.

Lord, don't let me do anything really stupid.

"Go to the head of the line," said the clipboard lady. "Your number is 45, the lowest number in this group."

The emcee at the podium a block or two away, it seemed anyway, called for attention, welcoming everyone. "Judges, take your places, please."

Eight men and women stepped down from the stage to stand with their clipboards, two of them per side.

The clipboard lady tapped Michael on his shoulder with an "Off you go and good luck."

Michael winked at me. "Head up, stretch tall, smile."

To the center of the floor we went. He stopped, brought me around to face him. I placed my arms on his. He grinned. "You look real pretty, Miss Thea. Let's do it."

The throb of the waltz beat began. "Go, forty-five!" I heard someone shout.

That's us. Adrenaline rushed through me, and I stretched taller. Michael reacted and twirled me in a wide outside turn. My skirts swishing, feathers a-flying, moving with the speed of a strobe, we spun around the room. Oh, happy days.

"Go, Thea. You can do it!" I heard Patty shout as we waltzed by her. I felt as though the sun had emerged from a cloud and spotlighted me. I heard angelic music, in waltz time.

I danced the rest of the heats that evening in a haze. I'd been in two semi-finals, the Newcomers waltz and Beginners tango, which meant I'd actually danced ten times in twenty minutes. Finally, all the heats for those two divisions were finished and the public had been offered two general dances.

The judges were ready to award the prizes.

"Here we go," said Michael. And he hurried me to the center of the floor to join a semi-circular line of couples facing the stage. Three of the judges holding baskets of glittering medals planted themselves beneath the podium. Michael's cold hand closed over mine. "Smile. No matter what happens, smile."

I had no idea what to expect. The room quieted. In the silence I heard my name, "A First Place goes to Thea Clark and her teacher, Michael Jensen, Newcomers waltz."

Michael jerked me forward and we hurried to the judge on the far right who handed me a gold and black medallion the size of a quarter on which the number one was printed.

Now I got excited but when I opened my mouth to comment, Michael shushed me. "Listen."

The next heat's winners were announced. The emcee went through the First Places. Then, I heard my name. "A Second Place in foxtrot to Thea Clark and Michael Jensen." Once more, we raced to the trio of judges.

"Thank you very much," I said as I was handed a plastic medallion with a number two on it. Then we hurried back to our place in the curved line.

In the space of fifteen minutes over thirty prizes were awarded. When the now familiar judge handed me a First Place disk for American tango, I sang my thank you. "You did well," he said.

To be honest, I had no idea how I'd react to winning. I floated off the floor with Michael squeezing my hand repeatedly in his joy. When we landed at our table, Patty, breathing heavily after completing a Viennese waltz, clapped her hands. "You were great and look fabulous in that peach gown."

"Thank you for suggesting Lewis, I love what he created for me. I fanned my skirt and fluffed the feathers carefully as I sat. I was trembling all over with relief, my muscles collapsing after being on high alert.

Day one of my first big dance competition had ended. I was hooked.

19

The Dreaded Cha Cha Cha

"What happens next?" I asked Michael.

"We're finished for the evening. Why don't you get some sleep? The Latin and rhythm heats start at eight tomorrow morning."

"Wait," said Patty. "What are you wearing tomorrow?"

"Oh, I found a cocktail dress, a long sleeved shift of silver sequin material. Very sparkly. A wide silver organza ruffle around the hem." I laughed. "Everything glitters and bounces as I walk."

The next morning at seven-thirty, wearing the sequined dress and matching shoes and matching earrings, I made my way again through the hundreds of tired-looking all nighters. In the ballroom I realized I was the first of our group to arrive. Soon Patty appeared in her Latin costume of blue and silver sequins, with blue feathers at attention on one of her shoulders.

"I came to root for you," she said. "Turn around and let me see the total effect. Uh oh. That bow has got to go. Too big and floppy."

"This?" I pointed to the silver organza bow the size of a small pom-pom.

"Yes. It's distracting."

And before I could say 'Bob's your uncle,' she had whipped out a pair of manicure scissors from her dance bag and snipped off the offending appendage.

"There," she said satisfied. "Now, the judges will be mesmerized by your Cuban hip motion, not a wildly flopping bow."

The next voice I heard was that of the emcee calling for the Newcomers to line up.

We did. We danced, the ruffle rippled. My hips did their darndest on rumba and the meringue. I was doing fine.

Michael smiled confidently as we walked back to the clipboard lady. She pointed with her ball point to the head of the line again.

The emcee said, "Cha cha cha next."

I shivered involuntarily as we walked to the center of the floor, goose bumps blossoming on my arms under the sequins. I always flubbed the first step of this dance. In the studio I just began over, but I knew here that wasn't possible. If I got off time, I might not be able to get back on.

The music began. I stared at Michael without seeing him.

"Thea!" Michael called from a distance. "Arms up, smile."

I shook my head. I was too scared to speak.

"Thea," he hissed. "If you move your hips from side to side, I'll help you look like you are dancing. But you do have to wiggle."

I went blank for the ninety-second heat, only coming to when Michael tugged me off the floor. Thirty minutes later when the Latin awards were given out I gasped when I got a Third in cha cha cha. Either the dress had blinded the judges or the other women, despite their skilled partners, were incredibly bad.

By nine-thirty a.m. of Day Two, I realized that my first, and perhaps my only, ballroom dance competition ever was over. In the Latin/swing division, I'd gotten two Firsts, two Seconds, and two Thirds.

On the flight home, I wanted to dance down the aisle singing "I won, I won." I'd actually danced in front of strangers and not made a fool of myself.

Two days later, Michael called to say he was changing dance studios, one closer to my home.

Now what? And what would happen to the lessons remaining on my monthly plan? I found out later. When I refused to pay for the unused lessons, the management turned my account over to a collection agency.

20

Nana Disappears

My mother, whose independence and energy I'd admired all my life, changed drastically before my eyes. Her weight dropped from her lifetime 135 pounds to a bone-thin 110. The year before, she'd been diagnosed with water-on-the-brain, an unforgiving nerve and muscle degeneration.

That's when I hired Maria, a kind and a good listener. Nana regaled Maria with childhood memories in Worcester, Massachusetts, some happy, some not so. Nana's deafness was the result of her father's cuffing her ears when he thought she misbehaved. The eighteen nineties had strict ideas on discipline no matter how young. The loss of her hearing and the glaucoma now affecting her eyes had caused Nana to become increasing isolated. Her physical impairments were closing the window of her known world.

And later that year she suffered a severe stroke, necessitating around-the-clock care.

"But a nursing home..." I said one day.

"As it is, you'll have no life of your own," remarked a close friend.

"Sounds so selfish."

"Your life, married and unmarried, has always been your mother's. Her sun rose and set with you, no matter where you were."

I knew she was right, but still I felt guilty.

One summer day at Nana's bedside, I felt it imperative to tell her how much I'd appreciated all the attention and support she'd given me during my lifetime of struggles and successes. I pulled the visitor's chair close to her hospital bed. Touching her cold, still hand, I said, "We've been a long time together, Mother. We've not cried on each other's shoulders, but we've weathered tragedies and challenges. I know you've been proud of me at special times. I remember the glow on your face when I received my Ph.D."

I could see her breathing, but felt no response. I went on, "Our relationship has survived jealously and fear of abandonment on your part, and on mine, anger at being smothered. Here we are at a time in our lives when confession and communication is appropriate, but impossible, a paradox. One I can't resolve except in my own heart."

Another evening sitting at her bedside, I again spoke aloud. "Nana, I'm caught between wanting to continue lessons and worrying about securing my own future. It may sound selfish to you, but I enjoy dancing so much I don't want to stop."

I felt a slight pressure on my hand.

"Thank you, Nana." My heart sang.

21

Michael's Teaching Days End

ONE UNFORGETTABLE FRIDAY night my amateur dance career slammed to a halt. Halfway through his Country Western class, Michael had a coughing spell and signaled Tamara, his advanced student, to take over. He nodded his thanks, walked to the sidelines, and grabbed his dance bag.

I hurried to the cooler for a cup of water. Touching his shoulder, I handed over the full paper cup.

He said, "I'm sorry, Thea. I know you wanted to learn line dancing. And I'm the best." For an instant, his great grin reappeared. "But it takes too much energy." He started for the door. "Going home. Call you tomorrow, maybe." Slowly, he approached his car while I watched helplessly through the darkening windows. Backing away from the front of the studio, he turned the old Pinto around and disappeared into the night. My solemn reflection stared back. The class clogging the Texas cha cha behind me seemed unaware of the tragedy unfolding.

My intuition warned: dark times ahead.

22

Jealousy Was a Tango

For the next month Michael and I kept in contact by phone. He'd call maybe twice a week. I'd collect him for lunch at restaurants with home-style food, half of which he'd doggie-bag. Still he grew thinner. While he'd been slim when I first met him, now he looked skeletal, his cheek bones protruding.

One morning, his voice was so low and whispery I could hardly hear him.

"What's wrong, Michael?" *Other than the obvious.*

"My car got towed away last night."

"My God! How'd that happen?"

"I parked in the handicapped zone in front of the hotel." His voice took on a whimpering tone. "I had bags of groceries. Too many for me to haul from the lot across the street, down the block, and from the elevator to my apartment." He paused to take in a deep breath. His voice still barely a whisper, "This morning—no car."

He cleared his throat. "It's at the police impound lot."

"How do you know?"

"I called to report a stolen car."

"Oh. And where is it?"

"In Wilmington, near the Terminal Island freeway."

"And?"

"It will cost $365 to get it out—today."

Damn!

"It has to be cash," he mumbled.

Double damn!

"They close at six."

I glanced at my watch. Shit! Four-thirty. *I bet they'll charge him for the weekend too.* "I'll be there as soon as I can. Have to stop at the ATM ." I had another thought. "Okay if I bring Jolene? You remember my granddaughter?"

"Of course."

Her calm presence would lessen my own tension. Jolene knew more of Michael's condition than my other family members. She'd babysat children of parents with AIDS and was not nervous around the disease.

She answered the phone right away. "Hi, Grandma. What's up?"

I briefed her on Michael's car situation.

"That's too bad." She paused. "Is he worse?"

"Be prepared. He looks very sick now."

After collecting both Jolene from her home in Wilmington and the cash at a nearby ATM, I sped east along Pacific Coast Highway to Atlantic Avenue in Long Beach. We searched for the ancient hotel where Michael lived. I parked on a side street, and the two of us hurried around the corner to the main entrance.

"Everything's gray, Grandma—inside and out. And it smells kind of weird."

"Leftover vibrations of thousands of people over the past seventy years. In the twenties, it was one of the finest hotels in town." I grinned. "Not that I was there then."

From the empty lobby we took the small elevator to the fourth floor. At Michael's door, Jolene peered back down the hallway. "It is quite a trek, especially for someone who's ill."

Michael opened the door before I'd finished knocking. "Thank you for coming," he rasped. "Hi, Jolene. Nice to see you." He held the door open for the two of us.

"Michael," I said, glancing at my watch, "we've got to go. No time for chitchat."

"Sure," he said picking up his leather jacket from an old couch.

"Here," I said, handing him the ATM envelope containing the cash.

He stared at it silently. His Bambi eyes looked into mine and he whispered, "Thank you, thank you very much—Miss Thea."

We returned the way we'd come, Michael trailing along. I said, "I'm not sure where this police garage is. Mainly junkyards in that area?"

No one answered me.

Ten miles later, not wanting to show my nervousness as I drove amongst the desolate acres of wrecked vehicles and unrecognizable metal hulks, I hummed. I guessed I'd seen too many scary movies, because I pictured unsavory characters behind every pile of unidentifiable junk.

The scrap yards all appeared similar while the addresses were barely visible. I took a wrong turn. "Oh, Fudgsicles. Ten to six. "Where is that damn place?"

Suddenly, we saw the police logo wired to a chain link fence, behind which stretched acres of vehicles with numbered tags, many faded to almost illegibility.

My tires spit gravel as I yanked the Camry into the driveway at five to six. Brakes squealing when I pulled to a stop next to the office door.

"Thanks," Michael said. He opened the car door and hurried up the steps. Jolene and I sat not speaking. If I'd been a nail biter, mine would be down to the quick.

From a side door of the building a uniformed man appeared, holding a bunch of keys.

Michael waved a paper from the doorway. The guard pointed to a nearby parking slot. Michael spied his Pinto, strode as quickly as he was able to unlock the driver's side and got in. He started the engine then pulled up even with me. He stretched his arm out the window; I did likewise without thinking.

Will I ever stop mirroring his movements.

He dropped something shiny in my hand. "Thank you, Thea. Thank you for this and all the other things you've done for me. I don't have much left besides this gold necklace. It's fourteen carat. I'd like you to have it."

The lump in my throat kept me from replying. I peered at his face, the grin gone entirely, the transparent skin now stretched tightly over his cheekbones. I was looking at the face of a person already one step beyond this too, too solid earth.

Only a month had passed since Michael and I competed in Las Vegas.

During those four weeks, he'd quit teaching and spent four days in the hospital. Though he no longer danced, we occasionally got together at a restaurant owned by one of his gay friends. He was always warmly welcomed; I was "that woman" who paid for the excellent dinners he barely touched. One evening over the swordfish with dill sauce, he surprised me. "Would you like to go dancing this Friday?"

Pleasure overcame surprise. I hesitated, a mouthful of fish delaying my reply. "Tell me more," I said, trying to control the half-chewed food and my facial muscles.

"Do you have Western boots?" he asked.

"No, I don't have Western boots."

"Then, wear closed-toed shoes. It hurts to get stepped on." He paused. "We're going to a bar here in town—a gay bar. Can you pick me up at eight?"

"Whoa! Podner."

He grinned.

"Let me get this straight. Are you saying you're all right to dance?" *His cheeks are rosier, his eyes have more sparkle.*

"I'm feeling much better."

"Well, then. Sure. I'd love to go, although this will be a first for me. I've never been to a gay bar."

"Are you comfortable with that?"

Hesitating, I said, "I think so."

"Good," and he took another sip of wine.

Later, on my way home, I figured the invitation wasn't entirely generosity on his part. He probably needed to save money on gasoline and maybe, just maybe, he wanted to show me off a bit, too.

That night, once I'd parked my car in the bar's lot, he said, "Lock your purse in the trunk. You won't need it inside. If you want, I'll carry your lipstick and comb in my pocket. Drinks are on me."

Shades of those high school dates of the nineteen forties, and our coy habit of letting the guy carry our stuff. I followed his suggestion and headed for the entrance.

Michael held the door open.

"Whoa," I said. "Wait a minute. I can't see." I needed time to adjust to the dark barn of a room filled with men in Western gear. To my right stretched a highly polished mahogany bar, its brass rail shining like a gold comet. One side of the long room held clusters of tiny tables and chairs, while red faux-leather booths stolidly sat against the rear wall. A larger-than-usual dance floor straddled the center space. Lights from sound equipment blinked in the shadows of a far corner.

Michael still held the door open. The men standing at the bar turned their heads toward us checking our silhouettes against the twilight outside. Their faces remained blank until Michael moved to a shaft of light. "Hi, everyone," he said.

"Hey, Mike, how're doin'?" A number of those leaning on the bar straightened up and ambled over to shake his hand.

"This is my student, Thea Clark," he repeated to several men, three of whom he introduced as dance teachers.

For the next hour, though I was the only woman among forty or more men, not one made a flirtatious remark. Two of Michael's dancer friends did ask me to dance. He wouldn't pay them to dance with me, would he? Oh, what does it matter? They were courteous—and it was wonderful to dance with professionals.

At nine o'clock, several women in jeans, boots, tailored shirts, and Stetsons drifted in like a flock of starlings, noisily expecting attention. They, too, took no notice of me.

We sat at a tiny table next to the dance floor. His friends stopped by to talk, and often to ask for a dance. Not me. Him. Taken aback, I sat and watched the action on the dance floor. *So this is how it feels to be an outsider.* I'd become the invisible woman.

A heavy-set man in full Western regalia strode to the center of the floor, and attached a lapel mike. "C'mon, Folks. Time to do what you came here for. Even lines, everyone. Hands on hips and left foot forward.

No! Your Other Left Foot

There was a noisy rush to form four lines of men and women facing the bar. The crowd on the floor quieted, slouching at attention with hands on hips. The caller began a series of step descriptions and everyone moved in unison.

Michael motioned me to join him in the front line.

I mouthed a 'no'.

His lips formed the words, "C'mon."

I frowned at him. Everyone looked so practiced I didn't dare get in the line-up. I reminded myself of Van Gogh's The Absinthe Drinker sitting by herself in her Sunday finery. As I sipped my drink, loneliness dressed me in a drab costume. The music began and among the first row of eight men, Michael stood out in grace and skill. He looked ecstatic. When the music stopped, the caller announced a Texas two-step. Michael and someone named Paul remained on the floor, taking closed dance position, and as music filled the dark room, they began to dance. No one interrupted or joined them. Everybody at the bar and in the booths stopped talking to watch the two men glide and turn in each other's arms.

He's really good. Michael's really good, but how much longer can he do this? For the rest of the evening, Michael rarely joined me. Many men were eager to dance with him. When someone approached him with his hand extended, just as Michael did when he invited me to dance, I was startled to hear, "Michael, would you prefer to lead or to follow?"

This is a weird night. I do believe I'm jealous.

The following week a vigorous-sounding Michael was on the phone. "How're you doing?"

"Okay, and you?"

"Not bad. Did you have a good time on Friday?"

"Umm. Yes. Most enjoyable was dancing with you. Of course, I appreciated your friends asking me to dance. Out of courtesy to you, I'm sure." He said nothing so I continued. "So what's up?"

"I'm calling to invite you to the annual Gay Pride Parade in Long Beach. Have you ever been to that?"

"No. I surely haven't."

"I'll be performing with Paul, my professional partner. You saw us dance the other night. Portable stages will be set up in the park just off Ocean Boulevard. We'll be dancing following the end of the parade. Just walk to the park and you'll see portable stages. Our name will be on the small marquee of the first one you come to. I thought you and Tamara might like to experience something different. You remember her? My advanced student who took over my group classes?"

"Sure. A nice person, a vegetarian, into alternative medicines, right?" I remembered her as calm and serene. "You're training her to be a teacher, right?"

"I was."

I stopped by Tamara's apartment the following week. "I thought Michael was through with dancing," I said when she came to the door.

"Sometimes he calls me. When I can," she replied, "I go. Good practice. With his help, I got my teaching certificate."

"Congratulations." I gave her a big smile. "I'm a little jealous. You still get to dance with him."

"My husband's consulting business calls him away a lot. He understands Michael's situation. I'm doing something useful, something I enjoy. And, we keep track of Michael and help when we can."

Fifteen minutes later, we approached the Vincent Thomas Bridge over the Los Angeles Harbor. Soon we'd crossed a second bridge into Long Beach and travelled on Ocean Boulevard to a parking lot as close to the park as we could find a shady spot. Tamara had packed a lunch of vegetarian sandwiches in Pita bread and I'd brought a thermos of herbal ice tea and a box of shortbread cookies. After noting where we'd parked, we strolled to a nearby area of sidewalk where the parade would pass. The most moving group I saw in the parade were the parents and families marching as a group, carrying signs, "We love our gay sons and daughters."

When the parade disbanded, Tamara and I headed for the park and the stage where Michael would be performing. The day was bright blue, the air clear and clean. The park bordered the ocean which, as far as we could see, seemed calm and flat as stainless steel. The park's grasslands in vivid green sang, "It's springtime."

We set our picnic on paper towels in front of the stage with the poster announcement of Michael and Paul. All around us men sauntered by holding hands with their partners, and women strolled with arms around each others' waists. A small crowd had gathered near us, some sitting, some standing: Sunday at the Park with George and George and Georgette and Georgette.

Waiting his turn, Michael paced back and forth on the grass in front of the stairs to the stage. "Paul is always late!" he groused, chewing the ends of his fingers. "He just likes to make me bitch to show he's boss."

This was a side of Michael I'd not seen.

Then we saw him, striding toward us and waving. He had black curly hair to his shoulders and a Pancho Villa mustache. He covered the grassland swinging two dazzlingly white Stetsons. From five feet away he tossed one of them to Michael.

"Catch, Mikey!"

I heard a grumble from Michael before he yelled, "About time!"

The two men, both dressed completely in white, climbed the few stairs to the curtained area of the portable stage. The announcer called for their partnered solos and in tandem they paraded onto the stage like the vaudeville acts of old. Michael wore a pink neckerchief and Paul a blue, to indicate follower and leader. I had to forcefully set aside old taboos while watching the two men dance in the same closed waltz position I'd often found so exhilarating.

I had taken an instant dislike to Paul at the gay bar, but he was obviously an excellent dancer. He led Michael in turn after turn. In one sequence, Michael twirled ten times, one right after the other. They followed with three solos then bowed to loud applause.

I'd never seen Michael go all out before. His pale forehead dripped with perspiration under the zinc-white hat brim. My own body tensed with empathy. I glanced down at my hands to see them clenched tightly. The effort required of him was so tremendous that he limped down the few steps at the side of the stage. The crowd had dispersed. I doubt that anyone but Tamara and me noticed Michael's deflation.

How tragic to be so young and to lose your reason for existence! I could see that Michael truly lived to dance. It's one thing to lose your life, but to lose your ability to do what makes you most happy, to be denied what you do best, must be hell. Oh, Michael, I am so sorry.

23

Help! I'm Going to Kill Myself

ONE MORNING I OPENED my door to frantic knocking. Michael's apartment roommate begged me to let him come in. "Help me. I'm going to kill myself!"

I stepped back. Years of teaching junior high taught me to not be shocked easily. "Okay, Roberto, tell me what's upset you. Sit there on the couch. Calm yourself while I make some iced tea."

He flopped down on my white divan, his head in his hands, calling after me, "Michael has left me. I don't know where he is."

"I'm listening. Go on."

"His note said, 'I've lived a promiscuous life and I'm paying for it. Goodbye'."

"Obviously, you know he's HIV positive?"

"Yes. Actually, I know he has full-blown AIDS."

I filled his glass with a shaking hand. "Are you okay?"

He twitched a shoulder. "Oh, I've tested negative for years. I know how to take care of myself."

"Then why are you here? And, how did you find me?"

"I didn't know what else to do. I hoped you'd know where he is. Your address is in our personal phone book." He started to cry.

Oh, hell. I need a real drink. "Would you like some more tea?

He nodded, his nose dripping. He paced, sat down, then was back on his feet and strode some more. Finally, he said, "I'm feeling better."

By now, Roberto had been in my living room for four hours. In the meantime, I'd heard far too many details of Michael's life and much too much information about his sexual shortcomings that I cared to hear about.

I really need a pee break.

"Good. Why don't you go home now. Maybe Michael is there and wondering where you are."

He sprung up from the sofa and ran to the door. As he dashed out, he shot back, "Thank you."

I'd barely closed the door when the phone rang. I almost dropped the receiver when I heard Michael's voice. "Hi, where are you? What's happening?" I imagined him sitting totally depressed among packed boxes of soon-to-be useless clothes and other detritus of a lifetime. But no.

"Hey, Thea." His voice sounded energetic. "I'm hanging in. Actually, I've been practicing with Paul and I want to run something by you."

"Oh, your professional partner in the Gay Pride Parade?"

"Yes, next month in Minnesota will be the Gay Men's National Country Western Championships. What do you think about our competing?"

What? Am I hearing correctly?

"Are you still there?" he asked.

"Wow, Michael. I can't believe what I'm hearing."

"I'd like to go." He sounded so confident. "I think I have one performance left."

I knew he was asking for more than advice. I gave him the answer I thought he wanted. "I say go for it." Then, "How's your cash situation?"

"I think I can get sponsorship for most of the fees but a little spending money would be nice."

"I can help with that, but I'll want to hear all the details of your conquest when you return."

"You got it." I heard his old gleeful laugh.

Tuesday, following the weekend-long competition, he phoned. "It's Michael. Guess what?"

"You're back?"

"Yep."

"All in one piece?"

"Yep."

"Dare I ask how you did?"

"We did pretty darn good."

"How darn good?"

"We cleaned up." He roared. "Hee haw. We got Firsts in every heat we entered. Dagnabit. We WON the National Championship of the You-united States."

I gasped.

"You gotta come over to see the humongous trophy. It's

so big, wouldn't fit in my suitcase. I had to hand-carry it on the plane."

"I bet you got lots of funny looks."

He laughed. It was so good to hear him laugh.

The next day at his apartment, in the midst of Western costumes strewn helter-skelter, I admired the thirty-inch, silver-colored sculpture depicting two men in skater's pose, dancing side by side with their names engraved on the base.

"What do you think?" he asked.

"Truly. I've never seen anything like it. I'm really proud of you. Now, tell me how you beat everyone else."

He listed the number of heats, the semi-finals they danced, and the finals.

"I guess Paul is pretty happy about your success," I said. "You knew I didn't like him very much. I thought he purposefully worked you too hard at the Parade."

"Doesn't matter. We're finished. We broke up on the way back. He's sick too."

Suddenly, his shoulders sagged.

"What's next, Michael?"

Then, that dreaded word.

"Hospice."

A few days later, his whispery voice was like static on the phone. "Thea, do you have a minute to talk?"

I could barely make out his words. "Sure." I waited.

"I'm feeling really lonely and depressed. Time for me to

move. Can you and Luke help me?"

Deciding to voice my thoughts I said, "Michael, what would you think of moving into my spare bedroom?" I heard a cough. "Hospice is so final sounding. Jolene and Luke said they'd help you if you were at my place."

I heard an exhale. "I really appreciate how you want to help me. But, no thank you. I don't think you understand what's about to happen. I have to leave this Tower-of-London-place. I don't want to die here. Before long, I won't be able to walk from the elevator to my apartment. I won't be able to climb your stairs either."

Though I didn't want to hear more, he went on.

"I won't be able to control my bowels. I no longer care whether or not I eat. I'll be on a lot of pain killers. I won't recognize my friends and may go into a coma."

My whole body flinched. *NO. No!* At that moment, I understood denial.

He knew what he must do. So with the help of Luke, Jolene, and Tamara, we moved him to a second story bedroom of a hospice in the next city—a room overlooking a picture perfect English rose garden.

24

A House Is Not a Home When It's a Hospice

MICHAEL'S HOSPICE APPEARED to be a residence much like the others on the eucalyptus lined street. His new room in the California bungalow sported two wide windows bringing in the sun. Sadly, in his hospital bed he almost disappeared under the white cotton sheets. I felt sure the bed clothes must be like sandpaper on his poor vulnerable skin.

"Good to see you," he said. His eyes traveled to my purse.

"Are you really glad to see me, or what I might have brought?" I shook my head. "I don't know why I'm doing this. Tell me why I'm bringing you Marlboros when you're so sick?"

He shrugged. I handed him the pack with a book of matches and had the feeling he couldn't wait for me to leave so he could light up.

"You know," he said, "we've never discussed what you'll do after I'm gone."

I stood very still, then held up a warning hand.

"Thea." He sounded impatient. "I know you still want to dance. No, don't deny it. Don't worry about being disloyal either. No time." He glanced past me out the window to the garden below. "Call Lewis. Do you still have his number?"

"Yes."

"Okay," he said with his old drawl. "Call him today. He'd

be perfect for you. Go home. Call him. Promise."

"But he only takes advanced students, right?"

"You won't know until you ask. One thing I do know, he works well with older women."

"Thanks. Thanks a bunch."

His laugh was barely above a sigh.

"I do remember he was all business when he made my ball gown. He's about your age, right?"

"About. He and his wife have a two-year-old boy. She's a teacher, too, you know." A hacking cough ended that conversation.

I waited until he quieted. "When we were in Las Vegas I saw them dance. They are well-matched, both tall and dark-haired."

"Call me when you've set up an appointment. I'll phone Lewis and tell him some things about you."

"Hey. Like what?"

"That you're a ham. Go." He closed his eyes. Visit over.

Sitting in my car under one of the ancient eucalyptus trees, I felt depressed in a way I had never experienced. For the first time in over a year, thinking about dancing made me sad. During those early months of learning, I'd been nervous, thrilled, scared, dedicated and joyful. But never sad.

An hour later, at home, my jasmine tea beside me, I opened my phone book to the "S" section. Taking a relaxing breath, I picked up the phone and punched in Lewis's number. *Maybe he won't be home.*

"Hello", said an adult male voice.

"Oh, hello. This is Thea Clark. Do you remember me?"

"Of course. How are you? Michael said you might call."

"This isn't easy for me, but Michael was correct. I do want to continue with lessons. He suggested I talk with you."

"Okay."

With trepidation I asked, "Do you take beginners?"

"Do you consider yourself still a beginner?"

"I've been in only one competition and two shows."

"Maybe you're ready for Intermediate? Are you asking for an appointment?"

This is moving fast. Breathe, Thea. "Yes, please."

"I use the P.V. Ballroom in the mini-mall at the top of your hill," he said. Then, "I'm sorry to hear Michael isn't doing so well."

"No, and neither is my mother. I have two people in hospice."

"Oh. I remember she wasn't well when I was working on your dress."

I filled him in on her condition.

"I'm sorry."

"I don't know why I told you about my mother. I must have heard sympathy in your voice." I cleared my throat. "Do you have time available?"

To my surprise he replied with a gracious compliment. "I'd be honored to teach you. And, I have six o'clock on Mondays open. Would that suit you?"

Ooh. "Yes."

"Right. It will be nice to see you again, Thea. By the way," he added, "you did well in Las Vegas."

I felt swathed in a soft Angora sweater, warm and fuzzy all over.

25

Lewis Suarez

THE NEXT MONDAY, instead of walking up the hill, I drove the two blocks. I didn't want to arrive sweaty; I was nervous enough. Nosing the car against the tire stopper in front of the studio's massive windows, I turned off the ignition and paused to observe the action inside. Three couples were rehearsing Latin, undulating around the spacious studio.

Apparently, Lewis saw me get out of my car; he arrived at the front door just as I had my fingers on the handle. With a welcoming smile, he gently took my dance bag and pointed to his table. "Would you like a cup of coffee?"

"No. Thank you." I took the chair he offered.

"That's right. You're a tea drinker."

I smiled slightly, wondering what to say next.

He repeated, "I thought you looked great in Las Vegas."

"Did you really notice me?"

"I could hardly miss you. I know that ball gown intimately." He laughed. "By the way, did you get any comments on it?"

"Several. One from the judge, Chris Morris, when he stopped at our table to say hi to everyone. 'Great color!' he said. 'Who made your dress?' He smiled knowingly when I told him, you did."

"That dress works for you," said Lewis. "That's the way it's supposed to be and not the other way around."

"What do you mean?"

"Remember when I took photos of you and Michael the Saturday before Las Vegas and I told you to always dance the dress?"

"Yes. You said, a gown may be spectacular, but if it gets more attention than the dancer, its success is questionable."

"I've seen costumes that dazzled the viewer, but didn't let the wearer shine."

"Not this one. I felt wonderful, even glamorous. The dress gave me confidence."

Lewis smiled, his black eyes twinkling. "Just so you know, what did he mean by saying you were kind of a ham?"

"I used to clown around in my classroom just to keep the thirty-five twelve-year-olds' attention."

"Right. I get it." He held out his hand. "Well then, shall we dance?"

Oh, those wonderful words. We began with a foxtrot; I got stepped on. "Michael began differently. He would ask if I were ready." I knew I sounded petulant.

"You don't need that anymore. You have to be more alert to my body, not just my hands."

We danced the perimeter of the floor. Suddenly, he asked, "Are you holding your breath?"

I looked up at him.

"Yes, you are. I can tell. Don't do that. You need to breathe."

"I tend to freeze when I'm nervous."

"You're doing fine, but breathing is good." His smile traveled to his dark eyes.

We danced without music, then he stopped to say, "Hold on a moment while I put on some Latin." He walked briskly toward the stereo equipment corner. I stood where he'd left me in the middle of the floor, the other four couples moving around me.

He returned, holding out his hand.

"What's that?" I asked, meaning the music.

"Cha cha."

I dropped my arms to my sides. "I don't do cha cha."

"What?" His look was incredulous. "Why?"

"I flubbed it in Las Vegas. My face is still burning."

He laughed. "Is that all? Everyone has stage fright. Wait, I remember. You got stuck on the floor or something? You didn't move the first few seconds." He chuckled. "That's nothing. I've seen people so scared they fainted." His face became serious. "So tell me, what's the problem with the cha cha?"

"I miss that introductory step, get stepped on, and from there, I'm off-time."

He looked relieved. "That's fixable. Just follow me."

The music played another cha cha. Lewis moved me to the right in that first step and then back in the cha cha pattern. "See? You can do it."

"You made me do it."

"Does it matter? You followed my lead."

He's so different from Michael. He exudes energy and power. I realized now that Michael's strength had dissipated over the months, sometimes so gradually I didn't notice.

Lewis said, "I warn all my students that I fine them a dollar whenever they say they can't do something."

"You're kidding."

"No."

I laughed. "Okay."

The lure of the Emerald City still beckoned. I was back on my Yellow Brick Road.

26

Jolene's Fifteen Minutes of Fame

Though I was excited to resume lessons, Michael's rapid decline deeply saddened me. When I visited, I noted that his hospital bed was positioned at an angle and, with an easy turn of his head, he could enjoy the lovingly tended blooms below.

"Thea, could you open the window a bit more?"

"Sure." A cloud of rich rose fragrance wafted up and through the open window.

"Thea, look," said Michael. "They put up your artwork."

Opposite his bed someone had tacked on the wall the large collage I'd created to relieve the grayness of the old apartment. I'd covered a four-by-five-foot white cardboard with photos of the two of us dancing in Las Vegas, adding magazine pictures of gold jewelry, drawings of Country Western dancing couples, several cut-outs of flowers and lastly, angels floating in blue skies, a visual smorgasbord of his favorite things.

The week after that visit, my granddaughter Jolene had her fifteen minutes of fame when she was awarded Hero of the Year award. Sponsored by the Pediatric Foundation founded by Elizabeth Glazer, the two of them were interviewed by Harry Smith of CBS. Jolene related how for two years she'd baby-sat children of parents with AIDS. Travelling to New York, being on TV were perks she'd never imagined.

I watched the morning program with Jolene's family in my poppy wall-papered family room.

Suddenly, Jolene smiled directly into the camera and high-fived. "This is for my grandma's dance teacher who is very ill. "Hi from New York, Michael. I hope you're feeling better."

I knew Michael would be watching.

No! Your Other Left Foot

27

A Doppelganger Or?

Impatiently, I waited for Michael's invitation to visit again. Finally, he phoned, but it was only to tell me his family had arrived from out of state, a brother and his mother. "I'm pretty busy with them right now."

"That's great, Michael—I mean, that they're here with you. Shall I come over to meet your folks?"

"Umm. Not yet." He paused to take a breath. "I'll let you know."

I was puzzled by his response. Didn't he want to see me? Was I suddenly persona non grata? Why?

He changed the subject, "How are your lessons with Lewis going?"

"Fine. Thanks for suggesting him. I'll tell you all about them when I see you."

He cleared his throat. "Can't talk anymore." And he hung up without saying goodbye.

What was going on? Had someone disconnected us? Was there some kind of conspiracy developing around him, isolating him? Maybe this was my imagination. Then again, I was determined to be there for Michael.

Visiting my mother depressed me. Her condition was disheartening, had been for over a year. "Doctor, what does this diagnosis, water on the brain, mean?"

"Not good news, I'm afraid. A slow deterioration and loss of the use of her arms and legs."

My feelings were complex. I felt sorry for her deterioration, and guilty I could do little to slow that down. I was frustrated by my inability to communicate with her because of her deafness. I felt guilty because I hadn't told her enough times that I loved her. Because she was now mute, communication was no longer an option.

In her first year at the convalescent home, I visited her three times a day. The second year, I had to psych myself up to visit once daily. Every time I opened the main entrance, I was struck by the smell of urine masked by baby powder; that familiar odor still churns my stomach.

During the day when my mother's curtains were pulled to the side, I could see the varieties of roses climbing the wall opposite her window. Signs planted in the garden said that a committee of volunteers cared for the flowers decorating the one-story building.

Whenever her windows were cracked open, the aroma of Mr. Lincoln, my favorite of the dark red roses—actually the only rose I can identify by fragrance—drifted into her room and blessedly overrode the odor of ebbing life.

A few days after Jolene's moment of fame, I phoned Michael. His hello was faint and tentative.

"Are you up to having Jolene and me visit you this coming Saturday?" I asked.

His answer was a faint "Yes."

On the morning of the visit, Jolene and I drove the twenty miles to the hospice, each silently musing.

The two-story California bungalow, probably built in the 1920s, sat back from the shaded street framed by towering eucalyptus trees. The structure hovered like a fat brown hen among a flock of variegated fowl. No sign was posted indicating that the hospice was any different from the other houses on the street. I was surprised at the gloomy aura. When we had transported Michael's things from Long Beach, we concentrated on getting our loaded car safely into the backyard, so this was an unhappy surprise.

Jolene and I walked side by side up the uneven sidewalk, absorbed in our own thoughts. Ahead we saw wide wooden steps to the screened-in porch. Involuntarily, we both straightened to meet the unknown encounter ahead.

Even at sixteen, Jolene had the serenity of a person tried by sadness and disappointment but who'd decided to see the positive side of life experiences. I always felt calm in her presence. Perhaps it was her physical attributes, her comfortable plumpness or maybe the brown eyes shining behind her glasses, or her ready smile.

At the top of the stairs we opened the unlocked screen door and found ourselves on a veranda reminding me of my grandmother's, complete with forest green wicker furniture, the cushions covered in brightly colored floral fabric. An antique oak door stood sentinel, the upper half a decorated Victorian design etched in the glass discouraging full view of the dark interior. A placard on a small round wicker table requested that we sign in before announcing ourselves over the intercom.

While we waited for a response, I remembered my previous guided tour. "Looks just like a home, Michael," I'd said to him. "Rather masculine, most of the furniture and walls are brown and beige."

Today, I peered through the clear spaces of the lacy pattern of the glass to see if anyone had heard us. A light at the far end of the dark, wood-paneled hallway silhouetted a figure coming toward us. Tall and slim, he seemed vaguely familiar. Suddenly, a door to his left opened and light from another room spread over him like melted butter.

I stopped breathing. I whipped my head toward Jolene. The slender man was now ten feet away.

It was Michael!

No. It wasn't. It couldn't be. "Damn!" I said aloud. *What the hell?*

I pressed my forehead against the glass to get a clearer look just as the man reached for the door knob. The two of us fell back a step as he pulled the heavy door inward.

No smile enhanced the familiar features. Not familiar was the handlebar mustache, the cold dark brown eyes, and the long curly brown hair. Up close he didn't look at all like

Michael. He spoke. "I'm Michael's brother, his twin brother."

Sucker punched!

I let go of pent-up breath. *But he's nothing like Michael. Where's the mischievous sparkle? The wide Dennis Quaid grin?*

Holding the door partway open but not wide enough for Jolene and me to enter, he said, "Who are you?"

I was temporarily at a loss. He was so much like Michael; it was like looking at a distorted mirror image. I blurted out, "I'm Thea Clark, one of Michael's students."

Barely audible, he growled, "He's not seeing anyone but family—today." Then, as the door closed, I realized that he hadn't even bothered to tell us his name.

"Wait! Please. We're close friends. I called him asking if we could come."

"He's sleeping," he said over his shoulder. He turned back to push the door closer to its frame.

Quickly, I stuck my foot in the small opening. "Well, wake him up!" My ire escalated. "He said we could visit and we've driven twenty miles to get here."

With his hand on the door frame, this other Michael stared at me. "Too bad you came all this way." Still no smile or words of courtesy. "You should have called me first." He sighed. "My brother has good days and bad days. This is a bad day." He closed the door, pressing against my foot, which I hastily withdrew.

I was indignant, but my protests were directed toward a receding back.

"Grandma," Jolene said, "let's leave a note."

"Right." I bent over the small table, tearing a page from the guest book, wondering if Michael would get the message. I stuck the folded paper with a short message in a crack of the heavy door.

"I guess that's all we can do for now," I said, feeling confused and deflated.

By the time I reached the car, my anger was at a high pitch. I sat behind the wheel trying to calm myself enough to think what to do next.

Jolene interrupted my fuming rage. "Grandma. Why don't we go back in and ask for the manager? I bet Dr. Rob will remember you helping move Michael. Perhaps he can convince Michael's brother to let you see him."

Thinking *exactly who does he think he is?* I said aloud, "What a nasty man! Where the hell were these so-called relatives when Michael needed money, transportation, food and moral support?"

I'd been cut out of the picture. Someone had erased me from the collage I'd created.

"Jolene, I'll calm down and get my thoughts together then I'll call. Maybe his brother won't be there or he might even have gone back home, wherever that is."

But when I phoned, I was told by a kindly voice, "No visitors. I'm sorry."

Was he not to know that I hadn't abandoned him during his most difficult time? Eleven months I'd helped him. I was pissed with no place to vent.

A week later the flashing red light on my message machine foretold the ominous. Hastily, I dropped my coat and purse on a kitchen chair, and hastened to the wall phone. I punched the message button. A neutral male voice said that Michael had died a couple of days previously, and my name was on a list of people to be notified. No phone number was left for me to return a call.

How dare they? Whoever they are! All I could summon was anger. My body was beginning to feel bruised with the pain of loss.

I phoned the hospice. His body had been moved. Michael's relatives left no information. None. The manager was sympathetic, but said the family didn't want to be contacted. There was nothing he could do about that.

I felt as though I'd been physically abused.

Nothing more for me to do.

Now, I grieved for myself.

28

Bereft

Michael's passing left me without a mirror. For months I'd depended on him to reflect my blossoming as a dancer; I'd felt so wonderful floating in his arms around the floor. I'd romanticized those VIP evenings at the nightclubs. Dance fantasies filled my daily life with secret, albeit unfulfilled, adventures. The excitement unique to Mondays and Wednesdays evaporated. Now even the shared lunchtimes were gone.

Our relationship had not been all give on my part; true, I'd helped him financially, but in truth we were each other's benefactors. He'd gone beyond helping me to learn a proper foxttrot. He'd reflected a side of me no one had seen before, an image full of exhilaration, competitiveness and fierceness.

I vividly remembered that sunny afternoon when I first saw the tall, slim boyish fellow dressed all in white as he opened the studio's front door. I recalled how he'd smiled sweetly at "Barbie," and scanned down the long room to where I sat in a far corner. He'd nodded. My heart flinched when I recalled the grin that wrapped you in a hug. How I'd miss those long flirty eyelashes.

I asked him once what had gone through his mind when he saw me nervously tapping my foot.

"You looked like a nice lady. And, you were a potential customer, at least I hoped you would be."

What an amazing series of events had resulted from those strides he'd made toward me. Highlights from the past year zipped fast forward through my head. Oh, my. Dancing to a live Big Band at Avalon, Catalina, fracturing my tailbone when I slipped doing the Twist on a Caribbean cruise, and almost landing on my coccyx during that Christmas waltz. And, most memorable, winning Firsts in Las Vegas.

I had mixed feelings about not being able to say goodbye to Michael in person. Sadly, he might not have been recognizable. Or, like my mother, he might not have known me.

Six months after his death, I survived another fall. While I lay semi-conscious, I thought I felt his presence nearby trying to help me.

29

Master Teacher

THUS I BEGAN SEVEN years of lessons, shows, and competitions with Lewis Suarez, solid and strong, a man confident in his own abilities and comfortable with his own talent. His thick black hair was Cary Grant short. His black eyes shot sparks of humor as if all the world was his stage and he loved being there.

One did not tiptoe around Lewis; straight talk was his style and expectation. He was patient and caring. When he complimented me at the end of my lesson, his arms enclosed me in a papa bear hug. Yet, though I was more than thirty years his senior, he was always the boss. "In ballroom dancing, Thea, the man is king." He laughed. "Probably the only place."

The pre-lesson excitement I felt now was unlike the anxiety I'd experienced with Michael. On Monday evenings, I'd drive to the studio from work. It was the same one Michael had used for so brief a time. I found it a happy place. I never worried whether or not Lewis would show. If he couldn't make it, he'd call the day before and reschedule.

I'd only had four lessons when Lewis surprised me. "Would you like to be in a competition?"

What? Had I heard him correctly?

"You already have a ball gown for the waltz, foxtrot, and

tango. Why not use it?" He smiled at me across the table and waited.

"Um. I'm just getting acquainted with your lead." I scanned his face. "Do you really think I'm ready?"

He shrugged. "Why not?"

"Is that a dare?"

He replied, "I suspect you like a challenge. You might consider the idea. This particular competition is held at the LAX Hilton, easy to get to in about twenty-five minutes."

"When?"

"The first of May."

"But this is already the end of March," I said.

"Think about it. But let me know soon." He pulled out his monthly planner from his dance bag. "You might need some extra lessons because I'll move you up to Intermediate."

Wow! So fast.

Putting his planner aside, he held my gaze. "You'll need a professionally-made Latin costume."

Uh oh. Once more dollar signs flew around the studio. Bravely, I said, "I still have that silver shift I wore for the Latin dances at Las Vegas. Won't that do?"

"Well—no."

"That dress left something to be desired?"

"Well—yes."

My heart leaped toward a yes, but my checkbook raised its eyebrows.

"Okay," I said nervously into the phone two days later.

"Okay, what?" Lewis asked. "Oh. You mean you'd like to compete?"

I remembered he couldn't see me nod. My voice squeaked out an affirmative.

"All right. Do you have someone in mind for your dress?" he asked.

"Yes. I'd like you to make it."

"Great. Then, we need to shop right away. When can you drive with me to Beverly Hills?"

"Beverly Hills?"

"What I have in mind, the shops here don't stock."

"Well," I said, "I've seen the costumes Christina wears, but your wife has the ideal figure for those skimpy outfits. Still, a costume for me wouldn't need the same yardage as the ball gown, right?"

"Oh, no, just a couple of yards. But if you're thinking cost, probably with stoning and all, about the same as the ball gown."

Snap! My checkbook closed, trying to lock me out. *Sometimes I feel this hobby is out of control.* But self-arguments against leaping before looking were silenced by a small voice saying Go for it, Thea!

Lewis was waiting for an answer. "I said, would you like to perform a solo with me?"

This man takes my breath away.

"Like the one Michael and I danced at the Christmas benefit?"

"I'd rather have a new one, one planned for the two of us. Chris Morris, the coach who choreographed that waltz, will be here next week. I could set up an appointment. All right?"

Excitement sent shivers along my acupuncture trails. It was true, I'd been comfortable with Mr. Morris. "Lewis, do you think I can do all this, learn the next level of steps, and a new routine—all in four weeks?"

"Sure. You can do whatever you want to do."

"My head knows that; it's my feet that don't."

30

Another Route to Oz

At nine that Friday night, Lewis dimmed the lights for the weekly dance and played music for an East Coast swing. I was seated on the sidelines talking to new friends when Cheryl, one of Lewis's advanced students, said. "I hear you're going to compete at the Emerald Ball next month." Her eyes widened as she waited for a response.

"Am I crazy?" I asked.

"Maybe not crazy, but gutsy." She rolled her eyes heavenward. "You have a new teacher for a couple of weeks then enter a competition and even do a solo with him? That's pretty plucky." She laughed again.

Later that night, I did have second thoughts about where my hobby was headed but I shared those doubts with no one. I carried my questions, anxieties, and what-ifs in a small mental box, opening it only when I was alone in the dark.

My mother, who might have liked hearing about my joys and frustrations, could no longer hear at all. After her last stroke, her health steadily deteriorated. Her glaucoma worsened until she became completely blind.

Even so, I found some degree of comfort in describing my lessons when I visited. Sitting at her bedside, I'd hold her "good" hand and squeeze it for emphasis when I laughed about some mistake I'd made on the dance floor.

Now, she'd never see me dance and I felt guilty that I'd kept my enjoyment so secret for so long.

One day a close friend reassured me. "Don't beat yourself up about Nana being in a nursing home. She needs the twenty-four hour supervision and care you're not qualified to give."

I began to be indifferent toward her my mom and I was ashamed. Adding to these unpleasant emotions was the disgust I felt for being neglectful. I was miserable. Only on the dance floor, even if only temporarily, did those ugly emotions sweep away.

Lewis contacted Chris Morris for an hour-long coaching appointment.

The afternoon of the coaching, I said, "Lewis, I understand the need for a lesson from a coach but I still feel intimidated. I know they are also often judges. I'm not sure I'm up to learning new material under such pressure."

"But you had a coaching with Chris before."

"Yes. But then I was more naive about competing."

"So the more you know, the less confident you are?"

"That's about it."

"The coaches are almost always also judges. But they want you to do well. They want to help you do well. They choreograph routines that are suitable to your experience and talent."

Talent, did he say? What talent? Did he know how hard I had to concentrate to listen and learn? Was he aware that these are sixty-three year old bones I'm pushing in a foxtrot run?

Hadn't I told him I'd always been a klutz?

"Thea!" Lewis spoke sharply from several feet away, striding toward me. "Are you ready? Chris is finishing with Cheryl."

The ballroom was filled with people on and off the floor, most rehearsing for the next competition. I sat up straight, took a deep breath, then a gulp of water. Cheryl walked toward the sidelines, book-ended by the two men. Lewis took Cheryl aside to talk over some points of the lesson while Mr. Morris ("call me, Chris") lounged in front of me and told an off-color joke. I laughed nervously.

I wasn't too nervous to forget why I was there. "I remember you judging at Las Vegas. You were most kind to me."

Mr. Morris said, "You looked great in that peach color. I understand Lewis made your dress."

"Yes. A great job, right?"

"Right. Let's begin," he said, signaling for Lewis to join us. "By the way, how did the Christmas waltz go?"

"Fine," I said, "except for two glitches."

"And those were?"

"My right heel got caught in the marabou feathers bordering my skirt. Then, I lost track of what we were supposed to do and I had to follow whatever he devised on the spur of the moment."

Mr. Morris chuckled. "You've now learned one of the three cardinal rules for an amateur: trust your leader."

"And, what are the other two?" I asked.

"Don't think. Just follow. And follow, don't anticipate."

"Aren't they all the same thing?"

The two men looked at each other and laughed. Both held out their hands in invitation as Chris said, "Let's get started."

When the hour was over, I'd practiced several new steps and repeatedly rehearsed sequences or "elements." I was perspiring, but I felt good that I'd followed the directions to their satisfaction.

"Thea," said Chris, "take the video camera and film the whole routine as Lewis and I dance it together. Lewis will do your part."

"Just tell me which button to push and how to aim the camera."

From where I stood at the edge of the dance floor, I followed the men as they danced, avoiding other couples. They didn't need music. They knew what they were doing without it. When the three-minute solo was complete, they waved at me. "Stop filming now." I handed the camera to Lewis.

"Come tomorrow night so we can practice the first steps while they're fresh in your mind?" he asked.

"Sure."

At home that night, I told Luke about my plans to compete in the Emerald Ball and my nervousness.

"Grandma, I think it's great that someone your age is trying something new. Go for it."

And go for it, I did, in the midst of the chaos of rioting in the streets in Los Angeles.

31

Dancing In A War Zone

IN 1992, TWENTY-EIGHT YEARS after the 1965 Watts riots, our nation's eyes were once again focused on the City of the Angels. The Rodney King trial promised to be so combustible it was moved to a neighboring county. Daily, the media recounted courtroom details and played and replayed Mr. King's notorious beating.

The trial's outcome was a no-win situation. Either way the jury decided, in favor of Mr. King or for the prosecution, emotions would be volatile. For days, Southern Californians waited impatiently for the jury's verdict. Not having a TV or radio in my office I missed the actual on-the-spot announcement.

Driving home from work, I was preoccupied by thoughts of the next day's competition with Lewis. I listened to the tap of the waltz music I'd dance to. Caught up with narcissistic images of myself dancing, I almost fender-bendered the car in front when I turned into McDonalds. *Pay attention, Thea.*

At home I set the package of fast food for Luke on the kitchen counter with a note that I'd be back in an hour, then I hurried to the Palos Verdes Library six miles away to return overdue videos.

To save money, several of us from the studio had decided to make the thirty-minute drive back and forth each day. The plan was to meet Lewis at eight the next morning at the LAX Hilton.

Now, traveling the tree-lined Palos Verdes North Road, I pushed the car to the speed limit, winding up the southern end of Crenshaw Boulevard toward Silver Spur Drive. In the right-hand lane and around the corner, I felt the engine shudder then die. Those behind me honked. Fortunately, I was able to coast the few yards around the corner then close to the curb and out of their way.

The driver behind me pulled his Accord ahead of mine, parked, climbed out and hurried over to my window. He wore a three-piece suit, a brilliant white shirt and spectacles. "I don't know much about cars," he said after looking over the engine when I'd popped the hood, "but I wouldn't try to move it."

At that moment, a woman in an MG convertible slowed down and called out, "There's a garage ahead. Do you have Triple A?"

"Yes," Althea Clark is my name. Thank you," I yelled to the departing MG's rear.

Mr. Accord said, "My wife expected me home some time ago. With all that's happening in Los Angeles, she may be worried. I hate to leave you alone, but I'd better go along."

"I understand. You've been very kind." *Something to do with the King case, I suppose.* I pointed to a McDonald's across the street. "There's a phone booth. I'll call Triple A myself," and gave him my best reassuring smile.

When I saw a lull in the traffic stream, I rushed across

the near lanes, the green belt and in between cars of the opposite lanes.

I dialed the emergency number on my card—now, what do I do?—then I saw the tow truck lumbering toward me. I waved. It must have been sent by the lady in the MG.

The driver stopped, leaned out of his window and shouted, "You Althea Clark?"

"Yes, yes. Over there—my car."

The young driver made a U-turn at the intersection, drew up parallel, and yelled, "I have another emergency called in before you. Can you go back to McDonalds to wait—get yourself food or something?"

I nodded and waved him on. *Now, I am getting flustered.* I expected to be home and resting by now.

After a chocolate shake comfort food, I headed back to my car. It was completely dark outside and safer for me to cross at the signal instead of jaywalking.

In my car with the doors locked, impatiently drumming my fingers on the steering wheel, I wondered how much longer I would have to wait before my help returned.

"Are you Althea B. Clark?"

I jumped as a second tow truck driver tapped on my window. *Thank goodness.*

"Please sign this," he said.

I rolled down my window, wrote my name hurriedly, and returned the clipboard.

He parked his two-ton in front of my dysfunctional vehicle. Once up inside the cab, I heard the radio crackle. His face became grim under the bill of his Dodger cap as he listened. "I'm sorry but I have another emergency. A girl in a VW is stuck in a ditch on PV Drive North. We're short-staffed tonight. You know, because of the rioting in L.A."

Rioting? Something to do with the King trial? He maneuvered the massive truck into the line of traffic with my car hanging on behind like an unwanted hangnail. Down the dark and winding road, he drove. "There she is," and he pointed toward a small red car ahead on the opposite side. Finding a place to U-turn, he pulled the large truck ahead of the disabled VW. He climbed down, shut the driver's side door, walked around the Bug, listened to the short-haired teenager, went back to the truck, and removed a two-by-four. Placing that under her rear tires, he slid into the Volkswagen's driver's side and gunned the little insect. Up out of the ditch it popped and crawled onto the macadam.

The eighteen-year-old jeans-clad brunette, on the verge of tears, thanked the driver then got into her little VW and sped off.

Hopefully, now we'll go some place where my car can be fixed.

"You're next," the Dodger fan said. "We'll tow yours to an all-night station on Hawthorne."

We drove down the hill at twenty-five miles an hour. Cautiously, he turned into a brightly lit station just as the automatic garage door thunked into its metal track.

"Sorry!" said a man jingling a huge ring of keys. "I'm not

staying open any longer. Too dangerous."

"Okay," the driver said to me, "but we can't wait here. Where do you want your car to be kept overnight?"

"I guess at my regular gas station on Western. But they closed at nine." *Damn.*

Back up Hawthorne Blvd we drove, then over P.V. Drive again, to Western Avenue and San Pedro and at last into the gas station near my place. Sam—we were now on first-name basis—unhitched my car while I climbed down from the truck, removed my briefcase and coat from the back seat of my Camry, locked it, and slipped back into my still warm seat.

Tired and indecisive, I wanted to cry. *Don't be an old lady and moan and groan in front of this young man.*

I said, "Sam, we've been together so long, I almost feel as though I should invite you in for coffee."

He laughed. "Mrs. ABC, you've been a good sport. I wish you lots of luck tomorrow. Take care when you drive into L.A. I don't want to have to rescue you again. Won't be much fun for either of us."

I felt a frisson of electricity travel up my arms. Stress nibbled at the edges of my nerves; my knees wobbled as I crept down the sidewalk. All the townhouses in my row were dark and shuttered. I unlocked my front door as quietly as I could. The blue aura from the TV bathed the room as I stepped inside. *Luke must still be up.* But he wasn't. He'd Scotch-taped a note to the TV screen on which some violent cop show played. "Call Lewis immediately," the note read.

I dropped my briefcase in a chair, went for the kitchen wall phone and dialed his number.

"Hello Lewis. Sorry to call so late, I..."

He interrupted me, "At last! I've been worried sick about you. Have you watched TV?"

"No. I just got home."

"Turn it on."

"It is on. Oh, my God! What's happening?"

"Riots," he said in a low voice.

With the remote, I switched from one channel to another. The same images: people running in the streets, throwing rocks, screaming at each other. Cars jamming traffic. Police everywhere. The noise! Oh, the noise!

Lewis said, "According to the maps shown on TV, many buildings on Crenshaw are on fire. I've called the hotel. It is just a few blocks from the main action." He paused. "The hotel concierge said competitors are arriving from all over the country and the competition sponsors have decided to maintain as if there were no riots." Quietly, he continued, "Your solo was scheduled for eleven tomorrow morning, but I'm not sure it's safe to travel then. I'll talk to the organizers tomorrow and try to get a new time. But, if I can't, we'll have to forfeit."

"That means I lose the fees paid, right?" *To say nothing of two expensive new dresses that I can't wear anywhere else. This is a stupid hobby!*

Lewis said, "I don't want any of my students in danger. In the morning, I'll call you after I've talked with the competition sponsors. Try to get a good night's sleep."

Sure.

The kitchen clock said midnight. I had barely enough energy to climb the stairs. Automatically, I laid out my street clothes for the morning, finished packing my dance bag with shoes and accessories. The costumes were already in garment bags in my closet. I slid a Tibetan chant into my tape recorder and tried not to picture fires and people going crazy, then fell into bed in my underwear.

Suddenly, it was six a.m. I sat up, awake and disoriented. I remembered last night, my struggles with the car and the troubles in L.A. My car. What to do about my car?

I was afraid to turn on my bedroom TV. What would I see? Bloody hell! How can we drive into that? If I still smoked, I'd have had a Benson Hedges menthol. Instead, I went downstairs to the kitchen, made a pot of jasmine tea, and sat mesmerized in front to the TV, saddened by the violent events I witnessed. I couldn't imagine the scope of the damage or how dramatically lives were being disrupted and traumatized. By comparison, a ballroom dance competition seemed frivolous.

I left a note for Luke with emergency information, telling him I wouldn't be home till one a.m. or so. The harsh ringing of the phone jerked me out of my reverie.

It was Lewis. "I'll pick you up in twenty minutes."

32

An Oasis of Elegance Amidst a Racial Tsunami

LEWIS RANG MY DOORBELl shortly after noon. "Seems safe enough," he said when I opened the door. "The others have left. You'll drive with me. We don't want to miss the banquet tonight. The professional cabaret show afterwards is always worth seeing. And you paid for it."

"I'm grateful you can drive me in. My car is still at the gas station waiting to be repaired."

Seated in his car, my costume in back and myself in front, I asked about my solo.

"Yes, I was able to reschedule. I'll tell you more about that later."

On the Harbor Freeway, we were relieved to see so very few cars heading north. Then, the infamous 405, which is often bumper to bumper no matter what time of the day, was even emptier. But Century Boulevard was a total shock. Like hundreds of tarantulas scrambling for a horde of flies, people of all ages swarmed across the wide boulevard with their rolling market baskets filled with whatever they could carry out of the electronic stores on each side of the eight-lane street. I sat frozen, aware of Lewis's intense concentration as he drove so very carefully, zig-zagging among the crazy pedestrians.

I'd never seen anything like this. *I'm afraid to get out of the car.* "There's the hotel, Lewis," I said with relief.

Inside the lobby, I found a different world, one seemingly unaware of the war zone outside.

Since we weren't registered for an overnight stay, we needed to find where we could deposit our luggage and change into our costumes. A sign in the lobby directed us to a conference room next door to the ballroom available to competitors. Opening the double doors to this huge room, we saw six-foot-high portable screens dividing the vast space down the middle. Women on the Left, a sign said. Cheval mirrors on rollers had been brought in, as well as numerous folding chairs and portable clothes racks.

"Do you have everything you need?" Lewis asked.

"I'll be fine."

"Good. I want to check on my other students to see if they've arrived. I'll see you in the ballroom, okay?"

I heard rather than saw the large double doors whoosh close. I was left alone, now the only occupant of the barn-like space, although it was obvious by the scattered debris many occupants had dressed and undressed there earlier. *Why is no one here? Is there a cease-fire in the competition? Oh, poor choice of words.*

Removing my street clothes, I laid them on one of the folding chairs scattered around the space. Nikes off first. Hard to get through the leg holes of the body suit wearing those size eight and a halfs. Carefully removing my peach satin dress from its garment bag home, I held it in front of me in order to step into the body suit. Gently, I tugged at the skirt waist to pull up the bodice and then insert my arms in the raglan sleeves. Thank goodness a trio of women walked in at the moment I needed help. "Hi. Could one of you help zip up the back? I'd be grateful."

The youngest competitor said sure, zipped me, and left.

"Thanks. Break a leg," I called.

The wide corridor leading to the ballroom was filled with costumed competitors, chatting with their partners, teachers and friends. To the left of the double door were four portable tables placed end to end. People seated behind them sold tickets to the evening event, checked in competitors who'd pre-registered, handed out goody bags, and answered questions.

I saw Lewis's dark head above the others in front of me. *Thank goodness, he's here in the ballroom. I honestly don't know what comes next.*

"Look over there in that line," he said as he approached. "Cheryl and Shannon."

They waved and called out to us. Even though they were much more experienced in competing than I, their wavering voices told me they, too, were excited.

Cheryl, an advanced student with a weight problem she constantly fought, was the best spinner of our group. I admired how she could turn so many times on one spot, required for the "spot" dances such as the rumba. She'd dressed at home in a soft grey-blue jersey with a full skirt and figure-flattering draping.

"That's a great color for you, Cheryl," I said. "I see you're all ready to go onto the floor."

"I don't like to strip in a room full of gorgeous bodies."

Tell me about it.

Each studio had its own reserved table. Ours was halfway down the left side of the room. Patty's blonde hair radiated above the others. Closer, I could see her sparkling smile and bright red be-feathered costume.

"Hi," Lewis said to Patty as she stood, giving her a hug. "Have any trouble getting here?"

"No. We came surface streets, along the ocean."

Opening his own booklet, Lewis asked, "Where are we now in the program?"

"It's confusing," she said. "Every few minutes the Master of Ceremonies announces cancellations and rescheduled solos, then it's a mad dash to flip the pages to keep track. Your names were already called. He read on when you didn't respond."

"I was able to reschedule," said Lewis. "Sunday. Six o'clock. We are the next-to-last solo of the competition." He sighed. "We'll close the competition."

Patty said, "Tough luck."

"Will there be anybody left in the audience by that time?" I asked. *And in what condition will the judges be?*

"I hope so," said Lewis, turning to the others. "Thea responds to people cheering. With her smile, she invites people to join her on her dance trip." He paused. "The judges like that."

"I really don't know what happens to me out there," I said, "because waiting to go on, I grow cold all over. My stomach cramps. But when Lewis extends his hand in invitation, something clicks into place. I enter a different space and time zone."

"You're right. That happens to many of us," said Patty.

Oh, I love being part of this elite group. Makes me feel important and special.

That first afternoon, we watched Beginner, Intermediate and Bronze solos in the Smooth dances. I was so nervous dancing with Lewis for the first time in front of an audience that I didn't remember much afterwards. I did okay, getting Firsts and Seconds. Lewis was pleased and gave me bear hugs at the end of every heat.

In the evening we joined the rest of the competitors at the banquet. "Seems sacrilegious to be eating gourmet food in an elegantly decorated room with burning buildings outside," I said.

"I agree," said Patty. "But, I don't even know what to do other than continuing."

"It's a 'damned if you do, damned if you don't' situation," said Cheryl.

"There's not much we can do about what's happening out there," said Lewis. "Let's just enjoy the evening performance." He explained, "Following the banquet will be a show by famous international dancers. Your banquet ticket helps pay for these champions. This evening's show will be champions from Italy. You know, many European couples begin dancing with each other as children."

"Really. Do they become life-long partners?"

"You mean like Christina and me?" He smiled. "Listen. The show's about to begin."

The elegant and glamorous couple began a flowing foxtrot to a Frank Sinatra standard. *I remembered Lewis saying once, You can always dance to ol' Blue Eyes. He sings in strict time.*

Following enthusiastic applause, the couple left the floor to change costumes. Next, they performed a saucy cha cha. They were "ten" dancers, meaning that they competed in all the smooth dances: waltz, foxtrot, tango, and the Latin styles of rumba, cha cha, samba, including swing and jive.

"Oh, they were wonderful," I said to Lewis. "Seeing Fred and Ginger in the movies is lovely but nothing compares with the excitement that ripples through a live audience as difficult maneuvers are accomplished successfully." He agreed.

When the show ended, I gravitated toward the lobby to meet up with Lewis. He'd said his goodbyes to his professional friends and his other students. I was exhausted from tension, fear, and elation.

As we drove on the 105 freeway south, I said, "It's eerie--there's no one else ahead of us or behind us." It was early Saturday morning and all the lanes in both directions were totally empty. "Is this what it might feel like to be the last people on earth?" I prayed we wouldn't get a ticket or something worse because of the ten o'clock curfew. It was now after one a.m.

33

We Close the Competition

Sunday afternoon, Lewis and I drove in by ourselves. None of our group performed that day; they'd gone home the night before with their awards. I didn't expect to see them. Again, we were relieved to find the late afternoon freeway travelling easy. The rioting had lessened, partly because the public was urged to stay away from the epicenter.

Once in the lobby, I sat enfolded in a cushiony chair, chaperoning our luggage and watching Lewis saying goodbye to his professional friends.

"See you in Vegas next month!" one called out.

The energizing tension of the first two days had dissipated like air leaving a tired balloon. Lewis and I had hoped that some of the other rescheduled dancers might cancel their solos at the last minute so ours could be moved up earlier in the day. The couple following us did forfeit, so that made us the true finale.

At last the time came for me to change into my ball gown. Carrying all my gear, I moved against the emigration. The changing-room was empty now of all but discarded plastic bags, scattered hairpins, and lonely half-used spray cans.

I placed my street clothes in a neat pile on the single folding chair left behind when the rest of the furniture had been moved elsewhere. Gone was the camaraderie of competitors in various states of dress and undress helping each other zip, hook, and fluff, leaving me with a lingering nostalgia. On the previous days, the flurry of preparation and the small talk among strangers with a common goal had helped allay my competition nerves. Now, I shivered in this desolate arena.

With no one to help me pull up the zipper and fasten the hook, I had to leave it undone. I covered myself with my old denim duster, picked up my dance bag and purse, and left for the ballroom .

Gone, too, were the tables for ticket sales that had guarded the entrance. I hesitated at the threshold. Would I remember my waltz routine? Could I recall the first step? Did I have the energy needed for those intense minutes? And where the heck was Lewis?

Clutching my coat around me, the back of my costume open to my tuckus, I stood inside the double door, forlorn and solitary.

"Hello, Thea." A familiar voice startled me.

"Oh, my gosh! Patty. And Frances and Teresa. I'm so happy to see you all," and we hugged.

"We came to root for you," Frances said. She gestured toward her sister, Teresa, and Patty. Then, she said, "And, to help put you together." She took the dance bag from my hand, set it on the floor, and helped me out of my old coat.

"Oh, thank you." I stood stock still as she zipped and hooked the difficult fastener. "Thank you, all of you," I said "for coming back. I can't believe you did this. Again I hugged each one in turn. "I'm truly grateful. You may be the only audience we'll have."

"We'll take your things to the table nearest the entrance to the floor," Patty said, glancing around. "Where's Lewis? Oh, there he is at the door now."

My stomach did flip flops. *My, he looks handsome.*

Walking toward us with a smile, he glanced briefly at another ringside table where four young men sat, their heads bowed in what appeared to be a serious discussion. They were shuffling papers, consulting plan books and not paying any attention to the five of us.

"Lots of hiring takes place at comps," Lewis said quietly, answering the questions in my eyes. He checked his watch then gave it to Francis to hold. "Okay, Thea, time to line up."

Line up! What line up? It's just you and me.

A tremor went through me. This emptiness felt heavy, so different from a room full of milling contestants with an audience chatting and clapping. "I don't know, Lewis, if I can do this."

"Shake your arms to loosen up," he said, as he adjusted the neckline of my gown.

"I've gone blank, Lewis." Having a senior moment was not funny.

"Stay with me the best you can, we'll make it through."

How had he kept up his own energy after dancing with all his students at least a hundred times in the past three days?

And now this anti-climax.

The loud-speakers echoed my name, bouncing it around the cavernous space. "And next, Thea Clark with her teacher, Lewis Suarez, will dance an Intermediate Bronze waltz. Let's give them a big hand. They've waited a long time to perform."

All eighteen people in the huge ballroom applauded, and that included the four judges, the emcee, the waiters clearing tables, the four young men, and my friends.

"Smile," said Lewis between his teeth, and he tickled my ribs. He brought my left hand forward as though he were presenting royalty.

We bowed to all.

Bless, bless our friends. They shouted like crazy! "Go, Thea, you can do it!"

The first minute seemed interminable. I began huffing and puffing.

Lewis whispered, "Breathe, Thea."

The next ninety seconds flew by. Abruptly, the music stopped; the vast room became silent. Then, an explosion of sound as our friends filled the air with their clapping and yelling. Lewis and I bowed to the judges, the waiters, the floor sweepers, and to our friends.

It is over, all over. Relief flowed from my every pore. *Calm down, Thea. This dress is not washable.* My first competition with Lewis in the middle of a racial tsunami had ended.

Back in the "changing" room I exchanged ball gown for street clothes, left to find a place in the crowded lobby to wait for Lewis. I wondered what all the people milling around thought of Los Angeles and our troubles. What a story to tell back home, wherever that might be.

Lewis arrived bringing energy and finality along with his own luggage. "I have your evaluations from the judges," he said. "I had to wait a bit for those to be finished."

"Did Patty and the others leave?"

He nodded. He went on as though I hadn't interrupted. "Every judge wrote a paragraph or two about your performance. They all loved your dress. Don't snigger. That's important. Also, they all felt you had good technique and for your level and age, showed excellent stage presence and confidence. All important. Now, let's get out of here."

In the car on the 405 freeway, I spoke of all my awards. "Are you pleased with what I got, Lewis?"

"Yes. Actually, you won more Firsts and Seconds than I thought you would. I'd looked over your competition and estimated fewer Firsts. Some of the other women were just as technically able, but your smile and happy face tipped the scale."

"I saw one woman, very high style with a magnificent gown, look absolutely terrified. I was surprised she made it through the first waltz."

"No one can give you stage presence, Thea. You either have it or not. It's very special. The judges recognized it in you."

The explosive rage of the public gradually lessened as the ashes of the burned buildings cooled. At least it seemed that way to me once home and thirty miles away from the epicenter.

My lessons with Lewis became sweet pleasure, and that joy colored the days of my week. Despite whatever was happening with my mother, Luke, and my job, I had those Monday and Wednesday afternoons to treasure.

My habit was to visit my mother before I went to work, on my lunch hour, and at the close of my work day. She couldn't hear or see me but she did respond to my holding her hand and combing her hair. I'd tell her about my day. Only in the car on the way home would I release my tears of sadness.

34

I Dance for Fun and Friends

UNLIKE MICHAEL, LEWIS WAS CONSISTENT and dependable. My hobby settled into a routine and my dance lessons built a solid foundation for a new direction of my life.

As educational program coordinator for older adults, my job was to find and schedule classes, seminars, and events at little or no cost. One afternoon, watching a senior citizen during a private lesson at the studio, I thought, What if a dance class could be added to the Oasis curriculum?

At home, I rehearsed my "pitch" to Lewis. One Monday, when I arrived at the studio, I unpacked my dance shoes and smiled when Lewis joined me at our usual window table. "Lewis, would you be interested in teaching a class for seniors? For people sixty and over?"

His look was thoughtful. "What do you mean, exactly?"

Leaning across the table and touching his arm, I said, "If I could guarantee enough older adults to make it worth your time, would you teach an afternoon class here charging the seniors a nominal fee?"

The way he moved his eyes, I could see a sweet memory lingered. "I had a ninety-year old student in Arizona." He paused. "Sadly, she had painful arthritis, but when she waltzed, she seemed to forget."

"I can understand that," I said. And I could. *I have a few aches and pains myself that disappear when I'm dancing.* "Ever since the Emerald Ball," I continued, "I've been giving this idea a lot of thought. There, I saw women and men my age enjoying themselves during the general dancing. Here, I've watched you at work. You have a patient and courteous approach. You treat older people with respect. They . . . we . . . appreciate that."

"Thank you," he said simply.

"I've also done some consumer research," I said. "I found group classes for all ages in other dance studios here in the South Bay, but nothing specifically to attract seniors. I think there's an untapped market."

"I teach groups here on Fridays before the dances," Lewis said. "Anyone is welcome."

"But, I want to create a class to attract seniors in particular, to make them feel special. I don't have much of a budget, but I do have a copier, paper, and people to distribute fliers. And because Oasis is a not-for-profit educational organization, I can ask for free advertising in newspapers." I gulped and rushed ahead. "My birthday is coming up in a month. What would you think about my giving myself a birthday dance party?"

His black eyes flashed. "I'm with you so far. What do you see as entertainment?"

This is promising. We're already up to the program. "What if we offered a nostalgic return to the Big Band sound and the Afternoon Tea Dance of yesteryear?" *He's so young, does he know the word, yesteryear?*

Lewis opened his plan book and turned pages.

Taking a deep breath, I plunged on. "Perhaps you and I could perform my new waltz routine."

Moving his straight back flat against the chair, he contemplated me. He laughed, then nodded. "Yes. We could. But, that's only three minutes. However, if you're willing to take a chance on following me, we could do a free style foxtrot or maybe a combination of Latin and swing styles."

"Hmmm. You mean, I just get out there in front of everyone and dance?"

"Don't sound so scared. Pretend it's a Friday night. Besides, you're not alone, you know. I'm leading you. Heck, you've already been in a competition dancing in front of hundreds of people." He flipped the pages to July. "What date?"

"July 12th is my birthday. This year it's on a Sunday."

"Let's see." He turned more pages. "Okay. I'm available." He moved to his head to one side. "What if I could get some of my other students to do their routines?"

"Do you think they would?"

"I'll ask. It's always good for students who compete to practice in front of a friendly audience."

I wiggled in my chair. "This could be fun."

Later, at home, my stomach felt queasy; my arms shivered with goose bumps. *Gosh, what have I started?*

Beyond my family, no one else knew I took lessons, much

less had been in a competition at the LAX Hilton.

Also, I need to get permission to do this, and ask for a budget. A letter to the head of my organization, and the permission was granted. Fliers were distributed in local recreational centers and adult education programs. However, the next few weeks I was busy with a new summer schedule for the seniors and I didn't have time to worry about the far-flung effects of the event I'd set in motion.

No! Your Other Left Foot

35

Happy Birthday to Me

My birthday Sunday arrived with the celebrated California summer weather. I hadn't asked for RSVPs on the fliers I'd distributed around town, so I had no idea who or how many were coming, if any. I was praying that more than my family and the dancers themselves would show up.

That Sunday morning, in slacks and an old tee shirt, I filled the trunk of my car with donated champagne and soft drinks, then drove up the long hill. Parking in front of the studio, I looked through the windows to see my fourteen-year-old grandson helping Lewis hang decorations. Luke held the base of the ladder while Lewis climbed the two stories to attach streamers to the traditional mirrored ball.

Oh, I can't watch. Having vertigo myself, afraid of heights most of my life, I envied Lewis his courage.

"Luke, when you're finished helping Lewis," I said after entering, "I need you to unload the car and put the beverages and the hors d'oeuvres in the bar's refrigerator."

"Sure, Grandma," he said, still looking up at Lewis.

Climbing down the ladder, Lewis stood back, checking the distribution of the balloons and crepe paper streamers. "What do you think?"

Happily, I surveyed the room canopied by a silver and pink tent of streamers. Confetti and more balloons decorated the tables placed around the dance floor. I clapped my hands. "I love it all. You've done a spectacular job. How did you get all those bouquets of balloons to stay put as centerpieces?"

"Pennies." He laughed when he saw my puzzled expression. "I'll explain later. Now, I need to change and bring Christina. We'll be back shortly."

I knew he lived only a half mile away and he was always fast on his feet. Well, he is a dancer!

"I want to be back here when my other students arrive to rehearse," he added.

Earlier in the week he told me that his wife, Christina, and her student, Tom, Tom's mom, Patty, and Cheryl would all perform. For the finale, Lewis and Christina would perform a romantic rumba.

Luke stowed the ladder in the studio's back room and then hurried to my car to unload refreshments.

I noticed that Lewis had placed a stack of printed programs on the small round table we had planned to use for the guest book. *He's even added a tear-off for those who want to sign up for the class. Great!*

He walked out the glass door and waved goodbye, then drove off.

Luke stood impatiently near the door. "Grandma I need to take a shower."

"Okay, okay, I'm ready to leave." Glancing around one last time, I said, "Let's go."

I was turning right onto our street when Luke said,

"Grandma! Slow down! You went through the stop sign."

"I did?"

"Jeez, Grandma."

I hissed through my teeth, "I'm so afraid something will go wrong this afternoon."

"Chill," he said.

Once we parked in the garage, Luke shot out of the car and across to the patio door. Inside, he turned back. "Grandma, people are coming to see a show for free, drink champagne, and dance. They'll have a good time. Don't sweat the small stuff."

But old anxieties about meeting others' expectations surfaced. Just then the phone rang; it was my friend, Dr. Oda, who lived across the street. She must have heard something in my voice because she was soon at my front door with her medical bag. Quickly placing six acupuncture needles along the middle part of my skull, she said, "I'll see you later at the party to help arrange the food. Keep these needles in for a half hour. I'll come over as soon as you call and remove them. Please, remember," were her parting words.

"Sure." Sitting on my couch, my eyes closed, I tried to relax. Then I heard a key turn in the front door lock. In came my son, David, his wife, Nancy, and their two children, Tyler and Halley. The latter said in her seven-year-old voice, "Grandma, you look funny."

I remembered and made a face. "You mean the needles on top of my head?" I laughed.

David interrupted. "Happy Birthday, Mom!" And gave me a hug and a kiss.

Nancy and the two children chimed in "Happy Birthday, Grandma," as they presented me with cards and packages.

"Ooh, thank you," I said, as I responded with hugs. May I open the packages later?"

I saw a shadow of disappointment on the children's faces but Halley said, "Okay, Grandma."

"Mom," said David. "I brought my camera. Shall I go up to the studio and set it up?"

"Good idea. The manager's name is John. He's a grumpy gus, but I've paid for the afternoon, so ask him for whatever you need."

He nodded. "C'mon, team." And they all trooped out the front door.

I packed the car with my ball gown and two cocktail dresses all in their own garment bags, and the ever-necessary dance bag with everything else.

Dr. Oda phoned to say, "Stop by and I'll remove the needles."

"Sure," I said, and after hanging up I glanced at the kitchen clock. *Time to collect the sandwiches.*

At the deli section, the Latina in her lab coat and chef's hat stared at me as she helped load the cart with four large trays of turkey pinwheels, tuna salad triangles, and open-faced sandwiches of chicken and avocado. I didn't have time to wonder why she was frowning. Precariously balancing the shrink-wrapped trays, I pushed the shopping cart toward my car. Holding onto it as best I could, I unlocked the trunk. *Damn.* The wayward cart rolled toward the car parked next to me.

A middle-aged man unlocking that car, reached for the traveling basket as it wheeled by. "Do you need help?"

"Yes, please."

After closing his car door, he carefully lifted the trays off the metal basket and onto the clean towels on my trunk's floor then closed the lid. "There," he said.

"I'm really grateful. Thank you."

He blinked. "By the way, may I ask what are those spikes sticking out of your head?"

Oh, gosh. I rolled my eyes heavenward and cautiously touched the ends of the needles. Shoot! "I was supposed to take them out before I left the house. They're acupuncture needles to calm me." I added, "I'm performing with my dance teacher at the Palos Verdes Ballroom a couple blocks from here. You're welcome to come. The afternoon is free."

"Uh. Thanks." He scooted back to his own car. "But I'd better get these groceries home to my wife."

Sitting in front of the studio, I carefully removed the needles and wrapped them in facial tissue to dispose of later. Lewis had returned with Christina. Other parked cars facing the studio indicated that the rest of the students had also arrived. Lewis saw me unloading my car and hurried out to help. "I'll hang up your dresses," he said, and strode quickly to the dressing room.

My daughter, Karen, with Luke and her other three children, pulled her car up beside mine. "Kids," she said, "help Grandma." Luke opened the trunk and removed the sandwich trays, carrying two at time into the studio and depositing them on the long bar where Dr. Oda was already organizing napkins, paper plates, cups and flatware.

In the dressing room I reflected on the risk I was taking, and recalled facing six junior high classes with 180 new names and faces to learn in a week. That was nothing compared to this. Klutzy Clark prepared to look glamorous and graceful in front of people who knew her as anything but. I worried that my teacher friends of forty-some years would feel obligated to clap politely for me, while wondering, what is she thinking?

More important, would I motivate the older adults to sign up? How embarrassed I'd be if no one wanted to take the new class. Thank goodness I saw lots of people lining the sidewalk outside the studio. It was only one-thirty and the invitation read two.

"Luke," I called from the dressing room, "please unlock the front door so people can come in and get out of the afternoon sun."

Joining me in the dressing room, Christina changed into her brief Latin costume. "Lewis told you, didn't he, that I'll act as emcee?"

"Oh. Yes."

"He has a thing about using a microphone," she said.

Christina, almost as tall as her husband with similar raven hair, was a spectacular Latin dancer. *In my next life I'm standing in the line that's handing out long dancer's legs like hers.*

I slipped on my floor-length green chiffon cocktail dress, slid into new satin pumps, and checked my stage make up. Taking one last look at my reflection, I straightened my posture, parted the curtains from the dressing room, and surveyed the studio now filling up with older adults in their Sunday best. *Looks like a good crowd after all.*

They were met at the front door then guided to seats by my adorable grandchildren, ranging from the teenagers, Jolene and Luke, to the younger children: Christopher, Heather, Halley, and five-year-old Tyler, whom I saw offering his hand to a stooped white-haired lady. He guided the senior to a nearby table, standing by her chair while she seated herself. My heart was full; the scene was lovely beyond words.

I was grateful that my whole family had shown up to help. David videotaping, his wife Nancy and sister Karen acting as hostesses. Jolene took charge of the guest book. Luke, in his best suit, looking old enough to pour the champagne, stood straight and tall, ready to fill the plastic flutes on the tables.

Tables and chairs had been set up for a hundred and forty people. In no time at all the seats filled and the grumpy manager agreed to set up extra tables and chairs. At two fifteen, I crossed the polished hardwood floor to the corner with the microphone podium. I didn't have to wait long for attention. The hundred and forty people sitting, standing or sauntering, stilled their conversations. All varieties of hair color and styles framed expectant faces. Nineteen fifties fashions incarnate sat before me in a semi-circle. *How I want to forever remember this happy scene.*

Christine offered me the microphone and stepped away. I swept my smile around the room. "Thank you all for coming today. Lewis and Christina have planned an entertaining program. While their students may be classified as amateur, you will see they look very professional. Give them a hearty welcome when they dance for you. Sitting to my left is the staff of the retirement home where I now work. David and Danee, you must have made several trips with the limousines to get so many residents here."

They both smiled and nodded.

Uh oh. There's Adolpho "Toro" Benedetto, the eighty-year-old Casanova, who's been trying to get me into his room the past six months.

I shifted my attention to the rest of the audience. "I see so many friends who mean a great deal to me. Most of you don't know I've been taking dancing lessons, and with my teacher I've been in two ballroom dance competitions in Los Angeles." Doing a Groucho Marx imitation, I said, "Ha ha. I've kept my light under a bushel," shaking the ash from an imaginary cigar.

"But light up I do, when I dance. At least it feels that way to me. And, I want to share that joy with you. I discovered my life didn't lose meaning when I retired from teaching at Dana. I hadn't left my persona back in the classroom. At sixty-three, I've become a student again, which amazes and thrills me."

I breathed deeply and swept my eyes around the room again, then raised my arms in a welcoming gesture. "We'll begin our program with some wonderful Big Band music. So, get up out of your chairs, find a partner and enjoy this foxtrot by the great Glenn Miller."

About half of the audience slowly rose from their seats and grinned their way to the dance floor.

Taking Senor "Toro" by the horns, I floated over to Adolpho. "May I have this first dance?"

For a moment, he looked surprised. Then, with a wolfish grin, he creaked upwards and grabbed my extended hand.

"No funny stuff, Mr. Benedetto. This is just a dance." I smiled over his shoulder as if nothing untoward was about to happen. Then, I slid his hand off my rear to my shoulder blade.

When the music ended, he gave an old-fashioned bow. I escorted him back to his seat where, with a gloat, he straightened his rounded back and tipped an imaginary hat to me.

Next, Christina announced a waltz while I hurried to the dressing room to don my peach satin gown for my solo. Moments later, wearing my new crystal earrings and pink pumps, I parted the curtain. *This is it*.

Christina announced, "Thea will dance the waltz routine she performed at the Emerald Ball the Sunday of the Los

Angeles riots. This will be easier, won't it, Thea?"

I smiled. *Maybe, maybe not.*

The audience quieted.

Lewis had walked to the middle of the floor and stood there straight and tall, extending his right hand in invitation.

I was aware of my new tight-fitting shoes. *Pick up your feet, Thea. Remember, heel, ball, toe, heel, ball, toe.*

He turned me to a side-by-side position like skaters on the ice. We stood absolutely still waiting for our musical cue. "Smile," he whispered as he lightly tickled my side where his hand rested ready to move me in the opening high kick. "And breathe."

Dear Lord, let me make this first move, this high kick, without falling or getting caught in my hem feathers—again.

He led me in the planned routine all around the room, and I beamed happily at the ringside seats. "Good," he whispered. "Have fun."

Three minutes later, we'd finished my last underarm turn and bowed several times to enthusiastic applause.

Lewis had put me first on the program, as I was the least experienced. He knew I'd make fewer mistakes when I was fresh.

Later, I would dance two more times in free style, just like at the Friday night parties. I was taking a chance doing this in front of an audience. Generally, Lewis liked all dances for performances planned and rehearsed ahead of time.

He wanted to show the seniors what they might do in his class, and risked that I'd be able to follow him. Of course, the more I saw him with students, the more I realized he could lead anyone and make them look good.

Still in my peach gown, I floated to the stereo corner where Christina again handed me the microphone. "Thank you," I said, puffing a bit. "Now, Christina will announce the rest of the program. I want to say first that I appreciate Christina, Cheryl, Pat, Linda and Tom for performing today. And, as I might forget at the end of the afternoon, I want to thank everyone for helping put this event together, my family, my friend Oda, David, Barbara, and Danee from Harbor Terrace Retirement Community, and especially my teacher, Lewis Suarez." I extended an open hand in his direction and smiled. He bowed. I returned the microphone to Christina.

People came whom I hadn't seen for years. I was surprised and especially happy to see my mentor from my early teaching days, Betty Zorotovich, and her husband, Nick.

In between solos, when general dancing was called, my grandchildren danced too, with each other and their mothers. Luke served drinks, and danced when asked by several women. Lewis's students Cheryl, Shannon, Linda, Patty and Tom each received appreciative applause. They all appeared to enjoy performing their particular solos. By four o'clock hardly any food remained.

Next I introduced the finale. "Thanks to Lewis, his wife, Christina, and their students, you have seen a wonderful show." I led the clapping and added. But who said, "You ain't seen nothin' yet?"

Someone yelled out, "Al Jolson."

The audience laughed and I joined in, then I said, "Now, Lewis and Christina, my favorite professional dancers, will perform a sexy Latin rumba. Watch her backbends and on-the-spot whirling turns. Let's welcome them."

Lewis strode over to the stereo corner where Christina stood, and formally invited her to dance.

I love that part of ballroom dancing, the moment of the invitation. Let's play. Let's do this together. Nobody else counts.

I hit the music button and the tour de force of non-verbal intimacy began—the thrilling interplay of sexy body language with hot Latin rhythms.

The audience gasped, then pounded their hands together as wildly as their arthritis allowed.

And afterwards, always gracious, Lewis and Chris moved around the perimeter of the room shaking hands. At the other end of the room, Patty, Cheryl, and Linda, still in their ball gowns, gathered at the mike. Tom brought out a huge bouquet of red roses, handing them to me with a bow, and the ladies gave me hugs, leading an out-of-tune rendition of "Happy Birthday to You."

"This is the best day of my senior years," I said, smiling through tears of gratitude and relief. The program had been a success. A huge success.

No! Your Other Left Foot

I knew that the staff at the Harbor Terrace felt the event was memorable when no one slipped, dropped anything, complained about the food, or had any—umm—accidents. Accompanied by their staff, the residents chattered their way to the limousines outside. A hundred or so other guests lingered to converse.

Grumpy Gus was already stripping the tables of decorations not already pocketed by seniors.

I'd paid for four hours and that was all I was going to get.

"Oda, any champagne left?"

"No, and I even had to cut some of the sandwiches in half to keep the refreshments flowing," she said. "Those seniors were hungry!"

I'd been looking forward to a drink, maybe a toast to all of us. Well, we'd have to do it with water. "Thank you all. It was a great afternoon. I salute you."

As I changed back into my old slacks and tee shirt, a huge let-down took my breath away. Hurriedly, I crammed my dresses into their bags and began the transfer of all my belongings and leftover decorations to my car.

David announced, "We've got a long drive ahead, Mom, so we're going to start for home. Happy Birthday, again. I'd say it was memorable."

My daughter collected her brood and moved them toward her car. "Mom, I took black and white photos for publicity purposes."

"How smart! Thank you. I'll write a story to go with the photos and send it all to the newspapers to advertise the class."

Back at home and alone, I felt restless. Now I understood why after a performance Lewis and his students went to an all-night restaurant. *The adrenaline is still pumping.*

The next morning, I stopped Luke as he was about to leave for school. "I saw you dancing in between your bartending duties. You looked very smooth. Thanks for being such a good sport. Did you have a good time?"

He shrugged. "More than I expected to. I didn't really know what I was doing, but ladies kept asking me to dance. I didn't want to be impolite, so I did my best. Sometimes I just moved from side to side." He looked sheepish.

"I'm proud of you. I owe you. What would you like?"

For sure, I thought he'd want a new video game, but he surprised me and left me gasping.

"I'd like dance lessons."

That fall, forty-five seniors signed up for the September class. Neither Lewis nor I had an inkling that we were about to launch a program that would last an incredible fourteen years.

No! Your Other Left Foot

36

Luke Surprises Me

WHATEVER KEEPS LUKE AWAY from drugs and losers, I'm willing to explore. The year before, he'd started karate lessons and I'd been hopeful, but after ten months and three belts he'd lost interest. The instructor was disappointed when Luke gave up. Mr. Napolitano did say, "He doesn't have enough self-discipline. He's too intense, he'll burn himself out."

Dance lessons are more costly than karate. *Oy vey! I'm looking at another four hundred dollars a month.*

The income from my part-time job and two small pensions barely covered my own lessons. In addition, there were my mother's expenses. Though our savings account paid for the nursing home, unexpected extras always surfaced. What the numbers on the paper implied was scary. After adding in my new lessons, damn little was left over.

Maybe I will have to refinance my condo.

Yet, later that night at home, over a cup of my Jasmine tea, I made a decision. I climbed the stairs to Luke's bedroom and rapped loudly on his door. The cacophony of an aggressive video game seeped under the portal.

"Luke," I yelled, and knocked again. "Turn it down!"

I waited a few seconds. "Luke! Turn down the volume!"

"What is it, Mom, I mean, Grandma?"

"Come out . . . please."

He opened the door part-way. "I'm at a crucial place in my game," he said.

"Oh, well, then, of course, forget it."

He calmed down. "I'm sorry."

We stood facing each other in the hallway. "I've figured out how you can have dance lessons."

"Cool!" he said with his hand on the doorknob, ready to escape into his dark-blue walled haven.

I paused to give him time to ask how, but his response was, "Thanks. Can I get back to my game?" He gave me that impatient James Dean look, head cocked, eyebrows pushing against each other.

"You'll have to go at the same time I do," I called to a closing door.

"Okay," I heard him reply. "Is that it, Grandma?"

"Yes." I sighed at the typically curt exchange and returned to my own TV program downstairs, full of fragile hope that dance lessons would absorb his interest. Could I, should I have anticipated the changes in store for both of us?

Lewis's wife, Christina, answered the phone when I called the next day.

"This is Thea. I'm not interrupting a lesson, am I?"

"No, hi, what's up?" she asked. "First, let me say how much Lewis and I enjoyed yesterday. It was fun for us to perform in front of an enthusiastic audience. They were all having such a good time. Hey! I thought you did well on your solo. I know you were nervous."

"Did it really show?" I bit my lip. "Anyway, thank you very much. Wasn't quite as scary as parachuting from a plane." Then, I laughed. "I'm thrilled to tell you that enough people signed up for two senior classes. But, that's not really why I called. Do you teach someone as young as Luke?"

"Luke might want lessons?"

"Yes. I was flabbergasted after the party when he asked about them."

"Hmmm. Lewis and I were watching him and thought he might have potential. Are you asking me for a recommendation?"

"No," I said quickly. "Actually, I'd like you to be his teacher."

I knew that not everyone was willing to teach a rebellious teenager, but I guessed Christina would be his match.

"Okay," she said. "I'll come with Lewis the next time you have a lesson and teach Luke a few basics. Then you and I can talk."

Two days later, Christina worked with Luke for a half hour. Her dark eyes sparkled. "He takes direction well."

Maybe from you.

Chris, Lewis, Luke and I sat at a table chatting. Turning to me, Chris said, "He learns very quickly." Then, to Luke, "What do you think about taking lessons from me?"

He gave a thumb's up sign. "Cool."

His second lesson was a revelation. "Lewis," I said as we were waltzing, "I'm envious. He picks up the moves so quickly."

Lewis shrugged. "He's a teenager, not afraid to go for it. He has a good memory for patterns, and he seems very sure of himself."

I rolled my eyes.

"Christina's from a large family. She can hold her own."

As a rapid learner, Luke wanted to skip over the fundamentals. *Too easy for me, he seemed to say.* But Christina, being a professional, was good at the balancing act, keeping him interested while requiring discipline.

I hadn't counted on an unexpected bonus. The two of them developed a close connection. After lessons, he often stayed to talk with her. She didn't tell me what they discussed; she asked if I was comfortable with that. I was thrilled to have him confide in someone and told her so.

He learned so quickly and looked so "cool" dancing with Christina, that I wanted to show him off. "Would you go to the Friday night dance with me this week? It's good practice for you to lead different partners."

"Oh, Grandma. All the old ladies?"

"Would you go for my sake?"

"You do pay for my lessons. I owe you that." Then he smiled and punched my arm lightly. "I'm only kidding, Grandma. Sure, I'll go."

A month later, Christina said, "Luke is very talented. Have you ever thought about his competing?"

Take a deep breath before answering. Can I deal with all that entails?

So far, I'd been in two competitions, Las Vegas with Michael, and the Emerald Ball, both requiring transportation, hotel expenses and extra coachings.

Can I afford to double that?

What did I want to do? What could I do? What should I do?

I wanted this troubled teenager to feel good enough about himself that he would stay away from drugs. I wanted to show the other family members he wasn't an incorrigible trouble-maker. I wanted to show I'd made the right decision by taking him in.

What could I afford? Nothing. It was all a fantasy, anyway. I figured I might as well quit and take up Scrabble.

A week went by while I continued my own lessons and talked about Luke with Christina and Lewis. They were willing to help by giving me a discount. I thought this very kind, considering this was their livelihood.

"What about Luke's parents?" asked Christina. "I met his mother, she seems like a caring person."

"Yes, but his family is a bit strapped right now. Actually," I said, "they seem relieved to have the problem child out of their house, at least for a while."

Nana hadn't wanted me to take Luke in. Now that she was in the nursing home that wasn't an issue. I saw Luke at a crossroads and felt he needed unconditional love; I was unaware that this temporary rescue would stretch on for years.

Before the year ended, Luke and I competed in Tucson. Luke wiped out his competition and was awarded Best Male Student in his difficulty category. The judges looked him over and he got compliments from other dancers. He reveled in the spotlight.

Wouldn't we all?

Never could I have predicted this new twist on my road to Oz. Now, the two of us were traveling it together, though I wasn't sure who was the Scarecrow and who was the Tin Man. I hoped I was still Dorothy.

Christina was thrilled at Luke's success. He memorized quickly whatever she presented. At six feet he was able to keep his "frame," and not slump before the music ended as did so many beginners. He showed confidence and enjoyment as he danced. And, most importantly, he stayed on the beat.

The male competitor's task is different from the woman's; he has to remember the steps and anticipate how to lead, all the while being aware of avoiding others on the floor and keeping his partner safe. While his teacher/partner can quietly direct him, she can't be seen to do so and definitely cannot be seen to "back lead," in order to help him win.

Just before we'd left for Arizona, Luke surprised me with a new look. "Grandma! What do you think?" he asked with a grin.

A friend had dyed Luke's Hugh Grant hair platinum blond. I gasped. "You look like David Bowie!"

He laughed. "Just want to get the judges' attention at the competition next weekend."

Those four days of competition were emotionally confusing for me. I was both truly proud of Luke and, I'm ashamed to admit, jealous of the attention. Three of the judges told Christina that she had a champion in her arms. Even though I, too, did well—I won best senior woman student—I now shared the spotlight with Luke.

Finally, the irony struck home. I'd gotten what I'd wanted all along—and I was miffed.

37

A New Studio

NOT LONG AFTER the birthday party and the launching of the seniors' class, I had a run-in with the unpleasant studio manager. He'd never liked the idea of the seniors at the studio. He preferred renting practice rooms to professionals and competing students. I reminded him that I'd promptly paid the four hundred dollar rental fee he'd required, though as a regular student I felt I should have received a discount. Apparently, the studio's owner had other complaints because shortly afterward the studio manager was fired, and that wasn't the only change; because of a leak in the spa's pool next door, the ballroom soon closed, never to reopen.

Two months later, Lewis found a much larger and newer place where he could hold his classes and teach his private students. When the owner of the mini-mall heard about Lewis's expertise he asked his advice on redoing the second story space as a ballroom. Soon Lewis was designing and overseeing the installation of a $50,000 floating floor, the professional dancer's dream, cushioned and easy on the knees.

The studio had been open a month when Lewis wanted a favor. One day, after my four o'clock lesson, he said, "Thea, I need some help." He pointed to one of the ancient couches visible from the top of the stairs in an alcove.

"Sure. What's up?" I plopped down on the sagging beige sofa next to him.

"The owner has asked me to do a show for some visiting Korean businessmen and I'm asking some of my students to perform. Like a showcase."

After slipping my feet into street pumps and tucking away my dance shoes, I faced him. "You're asking if I'd be interested?"

He was sitting forward, elbows on his knees now, watching my face.

"When?"

"A week from today."

"Next Thursday?"

He nodded.

"Wow. What would you want me to do?"

"I'd like you to dance at least one of your solos."

My ego turned back the calendar to the Los Angeles riots and my waltz performance with him. I guess if I could dance in that tension-filled atmosphere, I could do a little ol' local show. "How long a program?" I asked.

"Half hour, more or less." He looked past me to the several dancers practicing for an upcoming San Diego competition. "I'll be organizing this for free. I'd like to make it worthwhile for my students and myself—use it as a dress rehearsal. I'm doing the owner a favor. And likewise you'd be doing this for me."

I'd finally understood that when we danced with our teacher, whether a showcase or competition, we paid for his time and the use of the studio space. This time, he was telling me there'd be no cost to me. I was doing him a favor.

A week from now! I only had two lessons a week, just two hours to rehearse three routines. Could I do it? I said to Lewis, "This may be a way to thank you for my birthday party." I smiled remembering its success. "So, count me in. By the way, who else has agreed?"

"Christina, of course," he said. "Patty. Maybe Frances, I'm not sure about Linda. The show will start around eleven thirty."

"What?" I squeaked. "Almost midnight?" I'd assumed it would be a dinnertime show. I pulled my eyebrows out of my hairline. "That's way past my usual bedtime."

Lewis said, "The banquet starts at ten."

"So, we're on after the food, not before?" I groaned. "You know Thursday is a work day for me."

Disappointment shadowed his face. He patted my knee, sighed and rose.

"Wait! I haven't said I wouldn't do it. Let me think a bit."

While I felt some guilt that Nana was now safely in that nursing home, I was grateful to have more free time. I remained musing on the sofa watching the aquatic fish ballet. I glanced around the huge space crowded with dancers, the carpeted alcove and lounge areas, the disco ball suspended from a large beam in the center of the space. *Admit it, Thea. You are doing something some people think is crazy. I think it's crazy.* But I loved Lewis's attention, especially when I performed as he expected. And I cherished the admiration of the other dancers who considered this old broad one of them.

I marveled at the transformation from office building to dance studio; the smell of fresh varnish and paint still lingered. Now, the ambience reflected Lewis's professionalism, his friendliness, and his compulsion for cleanliness. I'd practiced at other studios, some where the floors were grimy. I hated dancing on a dirty floor where my shoes would stick. *I sure don't pay a hundred plus a pair so my suede soles can clean somebody's floor.*

The professionals flocked to this new studio before the paint was hardly dry. They appreciated the floating floor construction. Not only was it much easier on their knees, shin splint injuries were practically eliminated.

The cathedral windows at both ends of the sixty-foot long space provided so much daylight that fluorescents weren't necessary. At night two large chandeliers glowed over the vast expanse while the traditional mirrored ball and roving lights lent a psychedelic charm.

When I first attended the evening dances at this new studio, the revolving multi-colored spotlights made me dizzy. "Lewis," I said, "when I look at the floor, it's like dancing in a pool of moving, melted stained glass. Gives me vertigo."

"You know the cardinal rule, Thea. You look down, you'll fall over. Your body follows your eyes. Don't focus on your own feet. Focus on me."

Time to give Lewis an answer about the Korean show. His face wore a patient but hopeful expression.

Will this extra event be too much to expect of this sixty-four year old body?

Lewis interrupted my thoughts. "The audience will be mostly beer salesmen and probably full of their own samples by the time we go on."

"That's just great! A full stomach and a pleasant state of inebriation. They'll never notice my mistakes." Pausing, then I grinned. "Oh, what the hell. Okay. I'll do it."

Visibly relieved, he became decisive. "How about your bolero routine? It's dramatic and sexy."

I beamed. I loved the pounding of the bolero beat, having conquered the long slow steps and the cat and mouse attitude. "Anything else?"

"Since each solo is only three minutes long, maybe a free style waltz or foxtrot, too. Just follow my lead like you do at the evening dances."

Sounds simple. Not. Very scary. Lewis had always emphasized rehearsing routines before performing them anywhere. This time he wanted me to trust him enough to follow him without a warm-up or practice. *Oy vey!*

38

The Korean Show

The night before the show, Lewis called me at home. "Thea, I'm sorry to ask another favor—and you can say no—but I hope you won't. The two other students who planned to be in the show are sick. Could you possibly add another solo, say, your waltz?"

"The one we danced at my birthday party?"

"Yes."

I waited. "Anything else?"

"You have danced your rumba routine in competitions." I could picture him lifting an eyebrow to a question mark.

"The rumba, too?"

"Yes."

My mouth became so dry that when I tried to speak, I croaked. "Anything else?"

He cleared his throat, "If we have extra minutes toward the end, could you take a chance on a free style, pretending it's a solo? No one but us would know it's impromptu."

Groaning, I said, "I suppose you need to know now."

"I'm printing the programs tonight."

Three solos: my waltz, rumba, and bolero. Then maybe, two free styles: foxtrot and tango. That's at least five costume changes and all to do by myself, at the end of a work day.

Nevertheless, my ego reared its head, was tickled by the idea that I would be the amateur star of a show. I questioned that Lewis felt I could carry such a responsibility. He must be really desperate.

"Chris is dancing with you, right?"

"Oh, sure," he said.

"So, the program consists of you and Christina then you and me?"

"Yes."

"No other teacher volunteered to dance with their students?"

"No."

"The three of us are it?"

"Yes."

The phone line vibrated with anticipation.

My whole body said no.

Suddenly, I heard someone say, "Sure. I'll do it."

Heaven's to Betsy, it was me!

Lewis released a pent-up breath. "Tomorrow, if you can, come early, we'll warm up, go through all three solos. You know your routines by heart. You've done them all in competitions. This will be much easier, no judges with clipboards tabulating your every move." Quickly, he added, "There is no pressure to do this."

I hate it when someone says that.

"Well, Lewis, I've always wanted to show my appreciation for my birthday party. I was so naïve at the time, I didn't realize professionals didn't do that sort of thing. Now, I know you gave up several hundred dollars in teaching fees, you and Christina both."

In a soft baritone he said, "I really appreciate your doing this—I really do. See you tomorrow night."

The next day at work, I fretted. *Can I do this?* At a competition, I've always had a support group: my family or other students from the studio. Who was going to help me dress—and stroke my ego?

List-maker that I am, with paper and pen, I began an hourly schedule of tasks leading up to the time I should leave for the dance studio.

Lewis had cancelled the Thursday seniors' class so he could arrange extra tables and chairs around the perimeter of the dance floor. I was thankful. Helping with the class as I always did, would have taken energy I couldn't afford.

During the five miles to the studio, I tried not to panic.

Could I change costumes in between every dance? And all of this at an hour of the night when normally I was cuddling up with a cozy mystery and two fuzzy cats?

From an upstairs window Lewis had seen me park below in the studio's parking lot. In a jiffy, he was down the stairs and helping me with the slippery plastic clothes bags. As he ascended the stairs in front of me, Lewis looked over his shoulder and asked, "Want to practice before you change?"

"I think I'd better."

He gestured with my garment bags toward the staff room. Inside, he hung them on the portable rack. "See you in the downstairs rehearsal room."

While the large second floor ballroom was filled with dancers, the smaller ground floor was not. "Don't need music, just walk through the steps," Lewis said when I reached the bottom stair.

We waltzed through one routine.

"That's fine. Now, let's try a bit of the bolero and rumba."

We were rumba-ing when he sighed, "Breathe, Thea. You're making mistakes. Relax."

Finally, he gave me a Lewis-bear hug and gently pushed me toward the stairs.

Up I went, crossing the short end of the huge room floor to the improvised dressing room. Once inside, I found a copy of Lewis's computer-printed program taped to the mirror.

Hot damn! First up, the waltz solo. With a shiver, I recalled that other waltz solo years earlier with Michael, the one where disaster hovered as I lost my balance doing a high kick. Michael's quick thinking had saved that performance. Would Lewis do the same? Of course, he would.

Get with the program, Missy. No more time for worrying.

I heard a tap on the door. "Ready?" he asked.

Inching open the door, I saw him give me a thumb's up; I responded with a weak smile. He said, "Christina will announce your waltz. Wait on this side of the curtain until you hear your name." He looked handsome in his long-sleeved black turtle-neck shirt and black trousers.

He's not wasting his elegant tails on this freebie.

Even after a full day of teaching private students and arranging furniture for the banquet, he'd managed to go home and shower, his black hair still shiny wet, or maybe he'd used that new mousse stuff, a boon to dancers.

Chris and Lewis were scheduled to dance Latin, East Coast and West Coast swing. She'd wear the same costume for all three—what there was of it.

Ordinarily, I was excited by the tension and drama backstage—the camaraderie of strangers helping each other, the mutual nervousness. Tonight was different. I was by myself. No one with whom to share anxious fears. No anticipation in competing with others. Also, I'd been in two competitions where I wore the same outfit for all dances. Tonight, I'd go on, bow, dance, bow, exit, and change everything down to my fishnet pantyhose, then re-dress in an entirely different costume, jewelry and shoes and do it all again, all in forty-five minutes.

I glanced around the unkempt room full of old costumes, battered folding chairs, stale-smelling ashtrays, and dog-eared *Dance Beat* magazines. Even though I spent hours at the studio, I'd not invaded this staff lounge, now my dressing room. I felt abandoned, a stranger in a strange land.

Abruptly, my energy fled. I gasped. Terrifying waves of anxiety surged upwards from my stomach. I plopped onto the couch—another refugee from the Goodwill store—my head in my hands. I pinched the flesh on my shoulders until

I winced in pain.

Breathe!

Rolling my head from side to side to relax, I tried to remember the old cliché about a journey proceeding one step at a time, but I couldn't even remember how it began.

Oh. The first word is "A." And, the second one is "journey". . . . Whew.

Get the peach dress out of its bag. Stuffing my legs into the bottom half of the corset-tight "bathing suit," I inched the attached skirt over my hips and up my torso.

At that moment Christina slipped into the room and closed the door. Flushed from her energetic cha cha, she said, "Lewis took over the mike so I could help you."

"Thank you!" I turned my back to show her I was having trouble with the usual zipper.

Working hard to tug up the reluctant fastener, she asked, "How're you doin'?"

"Truly, not so good, but don't say anything to Lewis."

The zipper up, the hook and eye fastened, she gave me a pat, then faced me. Nodding with understanding, she said, "I've got to get back out there." And she left.

Lewis had told the truth when he said the audience would be all men.

Peeking through the makeshift curtain just outside the dressing room, I counted over seventy laughing and loud-talking males in dark business suits. The noise competed with the nauseating stench of beer combined with garlicky Kim Chee and other highly spiced dishes.

Hell! Why did I agree to do this?

I rehearsed a dazzling smile.

Even that takes energy.

Through the slightly open door I heard Christina announce me. I did a pirouette and encouraged my full satin skirt to billow out, giving myself momentum to exit the room door and march in place behind the temporary curtain.

To serve as a stage curtain, Lewis had stretched a seven-foot silver plastic fringe from the top of the door frame to inches above the floor. The conversational breeze blowing throughout the ballroom fluttered the strands, catching some of them on the rhinestones of my dress.

"Thea!" A staccato whisper from Lewis snapped me to attention. "Focus!" He'd swept aside half the curtain to present me to the audience. Taking my right hand in his, he moved me forward then released the curtain behind me. He replaced concern on his face with his performance smile.

I responded with a grin of my own and he winked in relief. In side-by-side skaters' position, we moved to the center of the floor and, with practiced unison, we bowed to the boisterous audience. Wordlessly, I noted the testosterone swirling overhead on waves of cigarette smoke.

Lewis remained still, waiting for quiet and attention. Then, tickling my side, he moved me forward in the develope, the first step of my routine. The following three minutes unfolded in slow motion. Muscle memory kicked in, my heart responding to the musical beat overrode my nervousness. For this feeling of euphoria I put myself at risk of ridicule, criticism, or broken bones. *This is the moment, this is why I dance.*

The music stopped three minutes later. Thank goodness. And hallelujah. I'd gotten through the entire routine with all the steps in the correct sequence. We returned to the silver curtain. Lewis parted the strands and I remained in place, my back to the audience, my pulse beating a drum-roll in my ears.

"Bravo, Thea," said Lewis. "That was perfect."

Enthusiastic applause deafened us both.

"Lewis," I gasped and turned around. "Quick. Unhook and unzip me please,"

"There you are." He gave my shoulder a pat. "After Chris and I do an East Coast swing, she'll help you with your costume change."

With a tissue I dabbed at the perspiration on my forehead. I had barely enough strength to close the dressing room door. My legs trembled, the left calf cramping. Grabbing a bottle of water, I gulped several swallows. I knew I'd only a minute to rest. I sat slumped on the old couch, crushing the pleats in my skirt.

Applause and whistles exploded under the door after Christina and Lewis bowed following their swing. Chris rushed in. She took my blue sequined Latin costume from my arms.

"Here, I'll help you. Harder to get in and out of your costumes when you're sweating, I mean, glowing." Efficiently, she stripped me of the satin gown and held out the slinky blue dress down low so I could push my feet through the leg holes. She pulled up the back zipper, while I inserted my arms in the rhinestone-covered sleeves. Smiling, she said, "There, you're in. Anything else?"

I shook my head, breathed in deeply and took one last look at my reflection. In the form-fitting dress Lewis called demure, I saw only the slit to my left hip and the deep "V" neckline cut to my diaphragm. Was that me with the Titian red hair pouffed high above blue rhinestone earrings the size of silver dollars? I didn't recognize myself with the false eyelashes Christina had applied earlier. Flushed and breathless, I followed her out to the silver fringe.

Still to dance, my rumba solo, my bolero solo and two free styles, the foxtrot and tango.

I recalled the words Lewis said earlier. "Thea, relax on the free-styles. Your kinesthetic memory will take over. And, trust me, if you make a mistake, I'll fix it. Just don't make a face that shows you goofed."

Fifteen minutes to midnight. Each dance—three minutes—I have to last twelve more minutes. God help me. I felt like a marathon runner on the last leg of the race. Could I make myself keep moving, breathing, and yes, smiling?

My rumba routine ends with a low dip to the floor and always gets applause. Ordinarily, I pop back up gracefully. But this time I needed Lewis to pull and push me upwards.

As he brought me closer to his waist, my human forklift

whispered, "Are you all right?"

"I'm okay," I hissed, on our walk back to the silver curtain. He moved aside a handful of metal strands for me. I was so sweaty some of them stuck to my face. In a panic I fought the tinsel cobwebs.

"Thea, drink some water." He scooted me inside the dressing room and sat me down on the couch. "We can stop right now."

"No! I can do it. I can."

Lewis had experienced my strong-mindedness before. "Okay. You have five minutes to rest and change." And once more he left.

A samba beat vibrated the dressing room wall. I knew I'd better get out of the blue dress and into the peach ball gown for the last three dances. I forced myself to strip. A light knock on the door and again Christina ducked in quickly.

Her nimble fingers fastened the difficult hook. Then, she dashed out to join Lewis on the dance floor.

I have no business doing this kind of thing this late at night. I'm not twenty anymore.

Like diminishing rain, the sound of clapping faded. For the final time that night, Lewis parted the silver fringe, led me to the center of the vast space and swung me into dance position for an American tango.

When I'd first learned this militant and aggressive dance, I felt silly snapping my head to the left and right, required for certain steps. One day, I made a snide remark to Lewis about jerking my head, and he gave me a stern look and said, "That's called styling, Thea. Just do it."

But trying to appear arrogant and noble while executing quick kicks and fast fans, sapped my fading energy. I began to have trouble breathing. I slowed, sagging. I missed a beat. For the fraction of a second, I felt Lewis pause then he drew out the next step twice as long as it was supposed to be. I knew he was giving me recovery time.

Not only can't I breathe; I can't tell him. I have no voice. Oh, God! I'm going to faint!

I stumbled, turning my ankle. In slow motion, I collapsed toward the floor, my full skirt ballooning out like a silk parachute as I dropped on my twisted foot. I bowed my head toward the floor, simulating a dying swan. Lewis, ever the showman, clicked his heels and bent over my outstretched hand, kissing it. Helping me stand, he shifted his arm to my waist and we bowed together. Wild clapping and shouts in Korean followed us.

I couldn't have thought of a more spectacular finale, planned or unplanned. In the staff lounge I slumped on the couch, unmindful of tearing or wrinkling my costume.

Christina opened the door and stepped in. "Lewis is thanking the audience. Great job. Do you want to come out for a bow?"

Rubbing my ankle, I indicated 'no'.

"Thea, you need to ice that. Now, I have to go for the last number."

Tears of relief flowed down my cheeks. I patted my stage makeup with a Kleenex trying to preserve what had not been eroded by sweat.

Christina returned when her dance was over. With her help, I removed my costume and dressed in my street clothes while she packed my dance stuff. I slung the bags over my arm and walked out of the dressing room for the last time that night. The fat lady had finally sung.

"Wait." She stopped me outside the curtain. "Lewis will help you to your car. Don't move."

Strong food odors momentarily impaled me. My supper of a hard-boiled egg and Melba toast had long since exited my stomach leaving that organ whimpering and empty. Seeing me frozen as a statue, Lewis said, "Let me take your bags to the car. Or do you want something to eat first, a beer perhaps?"

"No, thanks," I mumbled.

His next expression was a mix of concern, gratitude and apology. He touched my elbow. "Thank you for tonight. And watch that loose corner of the carpet at the top of the stairs."

Finally, outside in the quiet, dark night, I took a gulp of beer-less air and brightened. Lewis held out his hand for my car keys, unlocked the doors and carefully laid everything in the back. He gave me a bear hug and tucked me into the cool upholstered seat. "Can you drive with that ankle? Do you want me to follow you home?"

"No, and yes I can. I'm fine, I really am." I offered my best reassuring smile. "See you tomorrow at the seniors' swing group."

He rolled his eyes. "For a moment back there, I thought you were about to collapse."

I grimaced and nodded. He'll never know. On the drive home I admitted to myself my stubbornness and pride had put me in harm's way.

Suddenly, I was hitting the remote button on my garage door with no recollection of driving the six miles home. I stumbled out of the garage, across the small patio and into the kitchen. Dropping my costumes and purse on the living room couch, I staggered up the stairs, pulling myself up with my arms to lessen the weight on my injured ankle. Inside my bathroom cupboard I found an old ankle support and used the last of my energy to stretch it over my foot.

At last in my bedroom, after peeling off all my clothes and leaving them where they lay, I crawled under the sheets.

Damn! I forgot to put on my PJs. Oh, the hell with it. I've changed clothes enough for one night.

39

Surviving the Korean Show

THE NEXT MORNING I awoke triumphant. I hadn't totally embarrassed myself after all. It was eight a.m., the latest I'd slept in for years. At the foot of my bed, two cats joined together in a meow chorus, singing for their breakfast. Pushing aside the bed covers, I gingerly placed my feet on the floor. Every arthritic joint protested. My ankle let me know it hadn't been just a temporary sprain.

However, by four o'clock that afternoon, I was back at the studio to help with the East Coast swing class. I found Lewis sitting at his desk near the top of the stairs. When he saw me, he left his chair to skirt the half wall and, holding me at arms' length, checked me out. "I was worried about you last night. How are you today?"

"It was just a minor sprain—the ankle I mean."

"I told Chris that I'd asked too much of you."

I sighed. "I asked too much of myself."

"Seriously," he continued, "last night you were stiff and difficult to move. You went where I put you but you had no body flight. I began to think you were holding yourself together by sheer will power."

"You read my body language, right? I should know by now that I can't fool you. To admit that I might have ruined your show was a hard thing to acknowledge." I stared at the wall clock above him, hoping to change the subject. "It's time for class."

"Hi, Thea," said Lenore reaching the top of the stairs. "Ready for swing?"

She doesn't even huff and puff and she is in her eighties.

We both flopped down on the old alcove furniture to change shoes. I had trouble getting my dance shoe over the ankle support.

Lenore asked, "What happened there?"

"I sprained it last night, but I'm fine now."

Lewis took over, giving a short summary of the show. "Thea did a great job last night. But let's start today's lesson. Line up. Ladies across from me. Men alongside me. We did basic steps last week. Now, the *sliding door.*"

My thoughts focused on Luke during the short drive home. I needed to think about his place in my life. Counselors suggested that school might be a lost cause; he'd used up three junior highs in the South Bay. His absenteeism, his fighting and his non-participation in the classroom assignments led eventually to his dropping out. His addiction to drugs and his drug-using friends threatened to derail him.

On the other hand, surprisingly, he took to the dance lessons. He liked Christina and Lewis and communicated with them on a level I didn't share.

"The problem is," Christina looked serious, "Luke keeps

me on edge. He's inconsistent. He wants to skip the fundamentals."

"I so understand."

"I don't like to bawl him out, but I have to sometimes," she said. "Then I see him retreat." She shook her head. "He doesn't take criticism well."

"Tell me about it." I'd wanted him to find something to feel good about; he'd been such an unhappy kid. His mother's divorce and remarriage, his loyalty to his biological father, all ruined his chances of assimilating in the new family dynamics. Apparently, I had not lessened his adolescent angst by taking him in.

At home one night I asked him, "Why do you take drugs? That's not the real world!"

He shouted back at me, "Reality sucks!"

Our discussions about his drug use ended with his leaving the room or even the house.

Had I found something that would lure him away from that worrisome lifestyle? He still cared more about gaming and his friends. But at best, dancing came second.

40

The Cavalry

My lessons with Lewis were the Maypole around which my life now orbited. I'd become part of his extended family. I found excitement and acceptance, ego gratification and creative expression. I was not about to lose all that for lack of money.

But what to do about Luke?

Then the next month, after another devastating stroke, my mother needed twenty-four hour professional care. The nursing home expenses drained our bank account. Again I thought of refinancing my condominium. Would dance lessons satisfy a financial bank manager as a basic need?

All at once, from a distant place, a hot air balloon floated down with the keys to Emerald City. An aunt I'd not seen in thirty years passed away and left me thirty thousand dollars. I was flabbergasted. For a time I kept this influx of money to myself. Finally, I told Lewis and Christina. And thus, we worked out a schedule of lessons for the next year for both Luke and me. I was ecstatic.

The surge of cash lifted my spirits. Like a shopper with an unlimited credit card, I splurged.

Unfortunately, at the end of that year, Luke decided dancing was not for him, and once more he returned to his old ways.

41

A Dip to Build a Dream On

While coaching sessions were not required, they were considered ideal for competing. "Coaches work with the teacher showing the latest techniques from the competition circuit," Lewis explained. "You've already had coachings with Chris Morris and Debbie Avalos, and now Enrique Ramon is coming soon. Would you like a rumba lesson with him?"

"Oh, gosh. I've heard about him. He's very strict." *Can I survive an hour with a strange man telling me how to be sexy? Sure I can.*

Lewis made an appointment with Mr. Ramon and I met the two of them at the studio the next day. We sat at our usual table and exchanged pleasantries. Mr. Ramon asked Lewis about my physical abilities. "How flexible is Thea's back?"

"What do you have in mind?" asked Lewis.

Uh Oh. If I bend over backwards, will everyone hear it crack?

Mr. Ramon said, "She needs to move up to the next category of difficulty. The judges have already seen her at her current level. Let's do something surprising."

Though I resented being talked around as though I wasn't in the room, I kept quiet; he was a popular judge, and

No! Your Other Left Foot

like Merrill Lynch, everyone listened when he spoke.

Dressed in my practice slacks and scuffed black practice shoes, I stood between the two men while Mr. R. mapped out an advanced Bronze rumba.

"Can she do a back dip?" asked Enrique.

Lewis shrugged. "Probably, though she's never done one."

I glanced from one man to the other. "What are you talking about?"

Mr. Ramon turned to me. "You bend backwards as your partner supports you. Then he swings you from side to side."

"Oh, I think I get it. This is a trust thing, isn't it?"

"Hey. I've never dropped a partner yet," said Lewis. "Let's move to the center of the floor and Mr. Ramon will observe us."

Three times I began the move, but afraid to trust Lewis, I pulled up too soon. It was clear I wasn't ready.

Lewis gave me a gentle hug. "It's not necessary to do that swinging dip now. Later maybe. I know you're a bit nervous because of working this first time with Mr. Ramon."

At over one hundred dollars an hour for the coach alone, I have a right to feel nervous!

"Althea," said Enrique, "let's do the dip without swinging from side to side and just lowering you to the floor. Okay?"

"Please show me," I said.

Mr. Ramon pretended he was me. The two men faced each other in dance position. Lewis slipped his left arm around the coach's waist. Enrique fell slowly backwards, his head tipped back, keeping his arm around Lewis's waist. I could see him anchoring himself while sliding toward the floor with Lewis supporting his back. Afterward he gracefully pulled himself upwards. "Voila."

"I wish I could look like that, but it will never happen."

"It's the old story of how you get to Carnegie Hall, my dear. Practice, practice, practice." He nodded sagely. "The dip goes in."

I'd observed over the past year that in competing and performing there is always an element of the unexpected, and often risk. But then, if we were always sure of the exact outcome of anything in life, would we even try?

Everyone's life has its dips. It's the rising up afterwards that brings delight and fulfillment. When Lewis and I were in position Enrique said, "Ready?"

I let go of Lewis' right hand to step to his left, while moving my own right hand to his spine. I found his belt, grasping it tightly to stabilize myself.

All afternoon and every time I dipped I wondered if I'd make it back up gracefully and not plop on my rear. But the old muscles came through, teaching me something new about myself.

I also found that successfully trusting another with something you consider precious, like your body, can be rewarding beyond measure. *Hey! We all want to be dipped. Right?*

42

The New Me

Joining the competition circuit caused ever-expanding ripples in my life. I began preparations a month before the actual event. What costumes could I use that I already had? How much would extra lessons and coachings cost?

Emotional and psychological changes I thought were invisible to my co-workers and friends surfaced when I talked about dancing. I became animated, remembering "Carpe Diem." I'd seized my day and changed the direction of my life; I'd rekindled my ability to learn. I saw with pleasure that my new hobby had interrupted my projected biological time line.

When dressed in my specially-designed costumes, I assumed a new persona.

Feel passionate about something.
Run, fly, climb, sing—dance.

A few weeks later on the return to Los Angeles from the Arizona competition, Lewis asked, "Thea, how's it feel to be awarded top Bronze woman student?" He sounded satisfied I'd done so well.

"Unexpected," I replied. "Also there were fewer women competing against me this time." I wasn't being modest, just a realist.

"True, but you really were better," he said. "And you've moved up from Beginner to Intermediate and even added advanced Bronze steps. Next year you should compete at the Silver level."

"Moving fast, aren't we? Are you sure I'm capable?"

How sure of myself am I really? I'll find out soon.

43

Arizona for Two

"Are you ready for another adventure?" Lewis asked one October afternoon.

"Is this a trick or treat question?"

"No."

I paid attention. "What do you have in mind?"

"In December, the Holiday Dance Classic is held in Scottsdale, Arizona, at the Mountain Shadows Hotel, a beautiful resort in the foothills. We'd probably compete against my cousin and his ladies again. That was fun, wasn't it? Kind of a family thing."

"Arizona is your home, is it not? Good vibes? I never asked you about your entry to the dance world."

"I'd just graduated from high school and planned to be a medical tech major at a community college. Before the term started I saw a sign in a local dance studio: Wanted: Part-time teacher.

"And?"

"I always loved to dance and sing. I applied for the dance teacher job and got it. Been teaching ever since."

"How long ago was that?"

"Ten years. Of course, some months I don't teach full-time, but I've never quit my day job either."

"So, you teach here afternoons and are a night manager of a large store. Wow! When do you sleep?"

He laughed. "That's a good question. Yeah, my schedule is kind of topsy-turvy."

"So what new adventure might you be talking about?"

"Chris Morris sponsors this comp in Arizona. You remember him, the coach for your "Greensleeves."

"Sure, but what do you mean "sponsors?"

"Teachers, coaches, judges invest in competitions. They buy them to make money. Remember the one held in Los Angeles during the riots? That comp lost money because people were afraid to come to L.A." Lewis continued, "This time I'm driving to Scottsdale."

"I can see that would make a difference of several hundred dollars, but I wouldn't want to drive by myself."

Lewis said, "I have another student already signed up. Let me see if she'll carpool."

"Okay, I'll go." Now, I knew I was hooked.

Traveling in Shannon's brand new convertible meant I could be more casual about packing, and we could even take our own food. One afternoon during a light traffic spell, we left for Scottsdale. While I didn't know her well, I found her friendly and easy-going. Shannon had performed one of her routines at my birthday party, and with her good figure, a page boy bob and sweet smile, she was very attractive. After we were on the road awhile I offered to spell her behind the wheel, but she was so delighted with her new car she preferred to drive the whole way herself.

Across the border, mist from a recent cloudburst hovered in the air. She parked the Mustang in a spot near the registration area of the huge motel. Receiving our room keys, we returned to the car and drove directly to our assigned room in the next county, or so it seemed. We quickly unloaded the car and hung up our costumes then returned to the main foyer to meet Lewis and Christina for supper.

"Thea," said Lewis, "your first heat is at nine a.m. I'll meet you in the ballroom at 8:30 to practice. Okay?"

"Sure," I said. "Now's time for me to rest."

The next morning, the first day of the three day competition, the weather was spectacular, the kind of a day the chamber of commerce rushes photographers to local points of interest for the following year's calendar. Crystalline desert air praised a baby blue sky.

I gazed through the gigantic cathedral windows to the lavender mountains in the far distance. *For purple mountain majesties* came to mind. The gardens on the other side of the recently washed glass appeared layered in multiple shades of green. Exotic succulents and cacti offered their own unique beauty.

Soon I was dressed for the Smooths: the waltz, the foxtrot and the American tango. In our shared room I said, "Shannon, the sidewalk is still damp. I'm wearing my Adidas with my ball gown for the walk to the main building."

My old raincoat covered my costume and kept the satin skirt free of water stains from ceiling drips.

Finally reaching the ballroom, I saw Lewis already seated at our reserved table.

"Hi." I removed my rain gear and sat to untie the Adidas.

Lewis said, "Are you ready, Thea?"

"Almost."

"They've changed the schedule and called for our first heat. We need to get into the lineup immediately."

Still shoeless, I squeaked, "No time to warm up?"

"Just get your shoes on." He took hold of my elbow to help me out of the chair.

I stuffed my feet into the pumps and took a few steps.

"Why are you limping?" he said.

"I'm moving as fast as I can."

"Lift up your skirt, Thea," he said, glaring at me.

Shrugging. "Sure." *You're the teacher.*

He whispered, "You have your shoes on the wrong feet. Hold on to me. I'll change them for you." With both feet back on the floor, I stood while he hurriedly smoothed my feathers and tugged me along to the lineup.

Perhaps that incident broke the tension, for I did well in all the heats I entered.

I think I'm getting the hang of this competition thing.

Or maybe not, because a rough spot would surface the next day.

With some free time that afternoon, I wandered around the luxurious hotel. In the gift shop, I bought a pair of eyelashes that were an exact match to my freshly-dyed auburn hair. The next day when I was completely dressed for the Latin dances, I remembered the phony lashes, read the directions and began to apply them. But without my glasses, I struggled to attach the first of the fuzzy strips. By squeezing the kit's gray glue on my eyelid, I spread the goop with a toothpick and before it could dry slapped on the hairy caterpillar. At least I hadn't pierced my eyeball.

Shannon saw my plight. "Let me do that for you," and quickly had the second lash attached. She wore an abbreviated red dress with lots of fringe. "They look terrific," she said. "Your eyes look bluer than I've ever seen them."

"The lashes feel very weird."

We hurried down the corridors to the main building, again our costumes covered by raincoats. I used her as a guide as she walked ahead because I could hardly see through the bars on my eyes. I almost asked her if I could put my hand on her shoulder. "How do women wear these and not blink all the time?"

She shrugged, not really concerned.

At last we reached the ballroom, though much farther and I'd have needed a guide dog. I couldn't wear my spectacles because the lashes dragged on the lenses.

All went well during the rumba until the lash I'd attached came loose. It crawled its way slowly off my eyelid, pausing on my cheekbone. I was caught between paying attention to Lewis and deciding how to reattach the wayward eyelid appendage.

Instantly, Lewis sized up the problem and tried to brush the lash off my cheek with a stylized sweep of his hand. Didn't work.

In a millisecond, I concluded my best move was to feign passion.

I closed both eyes and trusted Lewis to know what to do with a blind partner and a drunk caterpillar.

When the music ended, I apologized. He laughed. "Hey, you followed great! Maybe you should dance with your eyes closed more often."

44

Goodbye to Nana and Michael

NINETEEN NINETY-THREE, a long year, one memorable for its extremes. By then Michael was very ill and in a hospice program. The highs centered on the competitions with Lewis, exhilarating jubilant times. In contrast, the lows: Michael's death in June and the rapid decline of my mother's health.

That autumn her condition seriously worsened. During my visits, she'd become more and more unresponsive. She was still my mother and the primary person with whom I'd shared the major events of my life. I continued to describe my dance activities and my feelings about my new adventures. These emotions were still new and fragile but I felt comfortable revealing them to her as she lay motionless, sadly making little impression under the white bed sheet. *My gosh, Mom, you're disappearing.*

Thanksgiving Day I stopped at the florist's near the nursing home for a bouquet of Nana's favorite yellow chrysanthemums. How many times had I placed fragrant flowers beside her bed not knowing if she could smell them or knew I was trying to please her?

Picking up the baby brush on her bedside table, I gently smoothed her sparse white hair. Softly, I told her I was on my way to Upland to celebrate Thanksgiving with the Cates, Shipmans, and Clarks. I sighed, patted her hand, kissed her forehead, and said goodbye. In the bed on the other side of the flowered curtain lay another white-haired senior in her own twilight zone.

It was time for me to enter the first of the four freeways I'd travel. Hurrying through the hospital-like corridors, I held my breath, trying not to absorb the constant reminder of the decaying condition of the inhabitants. Passing the reception desk, I wished the nurses a happy Thanksgiving. They offered professional smiles in return.

Ten minutes later I was headed north on the Harbor Freeway. The clear, cold weather reminded me of the autumn days in New England at my grandmother's home and those joyous times collecting red, orange, yellow oak, maple, and chestnut leaves from the trees lining our hill, Wigwam Avenue. I loved the Fall. In the months of September and October, I could see time passing through those chromatic changes.

After an hour, I drove into the cul de sac parking apron at my son's. No smog today hiding Mt. Baldy, the mountain to the north. I climbed slowly out of my car, then opened the trunk to remove the large tray of veggies I'd put together as my contribution to the dinner.

Luke, who'd come with his mother, saw me roll into the driveway. He hurried out the front door. "Let me carry that." As he grabbed the tray, he gave me a sideways hug.

My son, David, also quickly appeared. "Thanks for the

extra chairs, Mom." And, he too, gave me a warm greeting. "Luke," he said, "take these on into the house, please. I need to talk to Grandma."

Suddenly his wife, Nancy, was at his side. The air stilled when I saw her grave expression. She touched my arm. "Thea, the nursing home just called to say that Nana was bleeding from the mouth and nose. They believe she's hemorrhaging internally. They called the doctor, then us."

David took over. "I told them you hadn't arrived and I could speak for you. Was that okay?"

"Yes. Of course. Thank you," my car keys still in my hand.

He continued, "I told the social worker the family wants Nana made comfortable, but no extraordinary measures to revive her. Was that right?"

"Yes." Thoughts and feelings tumbled through my mind and body. Coming to a decision, I said, "I'm driving back to the nursing home."

By now, we'd walked inside where mouth-watering smells of traditional holiday food competed with hungry kids' voices. A hush spread over the groups as I moved past people who looked at me with compassion.

I nodded thanks repeatedly, but finally said as I turned toward the front hall, "I've really got to go."

Immediately, David said, "I'll go with you."

And Luke spoke up, "I can go."

"No. Thank you, both. This may not be the end. I'll phone as soon as I get back to San Pedro." I believe that I was confused about what I wanted to happen; I needed to be alone to figure it out.

"Wait!" called Nancy as I crawled back into my car. She'd put together a container of food and hurried with the Tupperware, giving me a hug as she tearfully handed it over.

Friends poured from the house to wave goodbye.

David leaned in the window. "You're sure you don't want me to drive with you?"

"I'm sure about that." Slowly backing out the driveway, I suddenly braked, stuck my head outside then called out, "Thank you, all of you."

The four freeways I traveled to San Pedro were remarkably light in traffic. I hardly noticed.

I was preoccupied with images of special times with my mother. She'd loved our weekend trips back and forth to UCLA my first two years there. I shared with her my classes, my grades, my difficulties and my successes. Though I lived on campus during the week, she'd collect me Friday afternoons along with my laundry. I was saddened by the comparison of then with now and despairing of what I'd find on my arrival.

The nursing home's lobby with bright bromeliads lining its entrance was cheerful and impersonal. I stopped at the receptionist's desk. "I'm Mrs. Clark. I'm here about my mother, Mrs. Bryant."

"Oh, yes. Please wait here a moment while I call our social worker."

My shoulders felt heavy and my throat constricted.

Shortly, a tidy petite woman walked briskly toward me, extending a hand, and inviting me to follow her. She stood while I seated myself in her tiny office before she spoke. "Your mother passed away about twenty minutes ago." She paused, folding her hands on top of her tidy desktop. "She didn't appear in pain. She just stopped breathing."

I felt as if I were standing on the edge of an abyss. What would my life be without my mother? I knew for months that death was hovering, but still my body went numb.

Mrs. Gomez said, "There are forms to be signed. Are you all right to do that now?"

"Yes."

She placed a thin stack of papers in front of me. The printed words and sentences melted together. I signed where she pointed.

"Your mother made arrangements years ago with Forest Lawn for interment in the family vault. Their people are on their way here. They will take your mother to Glendale. You can plan to see her there."

"Is that it, then?" I asked, wishing I could leave. "Thank everyone here for all their kindnesses to my mother." *I'll write a note later.*

Not ready to talk at length with my family, I headed south toward the ocean and my favorite "therapy" drive along the cliffs. Moving slowly over the winding single-lane road skirting the Palos Verdes hills, I thanked Mother for her years of love and encouragement. Tears flowed as I let the frustrations of our relationship wash away. My eyes roamed the velvety brown hills on my right, my vision softening as I recalled our first years in Southern California. How New England-born Nana loved the climate here, the ocean, the open spaces, and me. I'd been her total family while my father was away at sea half their marriage. She had loved me more than any other.

Did I tell her enough times that I loved her? Did I thank her enough?

Yes. But she would have liked to have seen me dance. I know it.

Okay, Nana. wherever you are, I expect you to clap and yell like crazy at my next competition.

45

Ramon, the Fearsome

CHRISTMAS WITHOUT NANA loomed heavily on my horizon. Her death left me disinterested in my surroundings and disinclined to change them. Lassitude demoralized me. Finally, with great effort, I pushed aside my grief and focused on a small glimmer of excitement, a huge competition in February, the San Diego Southwest Regional Championships.

Enrique Ramon, the well known judge and choreographer, came in from Texas and I was one of those fortunate to have captured a coveted coaching hour with the master. I recalled my first experience with him some months before; I'd dreaded his comments on my performance, yet quickly discovered that beneath his impeccable brown suit and stern demeanor beat a compassionate heart.

But on this December day, just a week before Christmas, I was frayed and fragile.

Mr. Ramon remarked on my lack of interest. "Althea, you're losing your frame. You know better than that." He tapped me sharply on my shoulder blade. "Get yourself a drink of water, while I confer with Lewis."

Sitting on the old sofa with my bottled water, I could hear them mumbling.

Mr. Ramon said, "This lesson is useless. She can't concentrate on what I tell her."

Lewis explained about my mother's recent death.

"If she's not ready to work today, there's no point in wasting her money," said Enrique.

Being stubborn, I wanted to continue, but I danced even worse than I had at the beginning of the hour. Lewis didn't comment, but his jet black eyes flashed.

"I'm sorry, Enrique," backing away from his attempt to put starch in my spine. "And I'm sorry, Lewis." I couldn't look at my teacher; the tears had begun to fall. I hurried off the dance floor to change shoes while I could still see my feet.

Lewis excused himself from Enrique, leaving him on the dance floor to talk with another couple, and cautiously sat down beside me. He took my hand. His gentleness and understanding were too much. I extricated my hand to close my dance bag. Straightening, I asked, "How much do I owe you?" He looked pained, but I knew he'd have to pay Enrique for the full hour. And, he, himself, should get his fee, so I wrote a check to cover both, tore it from my book and handed it to him. "Please say goodbye to Mr. Ramon for me." I was too embarrassed to do so myself.

Gathering my things, I mumbled goodbyes, hurried down the long stairway and out into the darkness of the parking lot. I sat in my Camry calming myself before driving the six miles home.

Luke was there, but not "there." Up in his room, he sat

playing video games oblivious to my comings and goings.

A cup of jasmine tea will soothe my nerves. I slipped into the VCR/TV console a taped version of the Ohio Star Ball, one of the biggest competitions in the country, and for some years the only one recorded for television. Drinking the hot brew, I asked myself what I was doing with this hobby. Soon I was mesmerized by the dancing on the screen and my mood lifted.

The next day, December 18th, when I called Lewis to apologize he said, "Don't worry about it. When can you come in for a practice?"

"Tomorrow after work okay? Six o'clock?"

"See you then."

46

Twenty-One Steps

At Dusk on December 19th, I arrived to find the first and second floor ballrooms packed with amateurs and professionals rehearsing for upcoming competitions around the country. My dance bag and purse seemed heavier than usual. I slowly climbed the long stairway. The old beige sofa in the alcove was a welcome sight and I sank into the stained lumpy cushions. I could see Christina and Lewis in the center of the revolving crowd. Dressed in their usual black practice outfits, they danced a sexy rumba. They finished with a flourish and, glowing with perspiration, ambled over to rest in the alcove a few minutes before they taught their next lesson.

"Hi," they said in unison.

"You two look wonderful!"

"Thanks." Christina smiled and dabbed her forehead.

"Lots of people here today practicing for San Diego," I said.

"Time for us to do the same," said Lewis, extending his hand in a soft command.

When my satin Latin shoes were buckled, I stood. He guided me through the whirling couples to the floor's center. Since rumba is a "spot" dance, we could occupy a very small space. Suddenly I slipped on a slick spot. I would have sat down hard on my backside if Lewis hadn't caught me.

"Thea, something's wrong. You're not paying full attention tonight."

"I'm okay," I insisted.

"Then, straighten up. You're slumping."

I took a deep breath and my body locked up, then I went limp. "Lewis, I can't lie to you. I'm feeling very sad tonight." Tears welled in my eyes.

"Do you want to postpone your lesson? Tomorrow or Thursday?"

"No, this is the week before Christmas and I have so much to do. The whole family always comes to my place."

Placing his hands on my shoulders, he held me still. "What do you want to do, Thea?"

His sympathetic touch triggered an emotion I didn't usually display. I shrugged off his hands and hurried to the old couch, plopped down, removed my dance shoes and jammed my feet into my street heels. Throwing on my old denim coat, I clutched it around my trembling body, bent over to pick up my dance bag and purse and started for the stairs, tears impairing my vision.

I heard Lewis call. "Wait, Thea. I'll go down with you." He must have been just a few feet behind me. "Wait."

At the top of the stairs I turned toward him. My body wobbled. Catching my heel on the loose carpet, I shifted weight, jamming my other foot downward. But I missed the first step, and walked off into space. I screamed, reaching for a non-existent railing as my side hit the wall. "I'm falling!" Then, I tumbled over and over, my dance bag and purse flailing, smacking the walls and me.

From a distance, I heard Lewis yell. "Thea!"

I bumped down every damn step. Semi-conscious, I heard muffled shouts echoing. I landed in an untidy denim bundle on the outdoor carpeting, the cement underneath, mausoleum cold. Bright Christmas lights outlining a full-length mirror to my right flashed on and off.

Thank God, I didn't crash into them.

Then I blacked out.

47

The Pain

Ouch!
Where am I?
I'm freezing.
Why can't I move?

I heard Lewis's voice at the other end of a dark-spinning tunnel. "Thea, I tried to catch you, but you went down so fast." His voice cracked. Fear emanated from him in waves. "Can you open your eyes?"

Aurrgh! Where am I? Is that a cliché?

Both eyes were jammed shut, my head pinned to a cold rough surface. Something prickly embedded my right cheek; I couldn't move my head. I forced one eyelid upward. *What is that moldy smell? Oh, yuck. It's that awful Astroturf. Not only can I not move my head, I can't move my legs. I can't feel my hands.* I tried to swallow, but couldn't. I had no spit, just some grainy stuff in my mouth. *Maybe if I open my lips—ow! Brain-freeze.*

"Thea." Lewis's voice was so close to my ear I could feel his warm breath. "Can you hear me? Oh, God. Are you conscious?" He didn't wait for my response. "Don't move. I hear the paramedics."

His cologne cocooned me as I wafted away to Never Never Land.

"See?" he rustled paper to get my attention. "I have your tooth in this towel."

I came to. What tooth? Whose tooth? I opened my mouth to ask.. Auurrgh! Oh, God. I've become "The Scream," that expressionist painting in all its howling color. My inner voice cried out. Move, try to move. I inched my head up, but fell back when the pain in my neck exploded, followed by a wave of nausea. *Can't throw up. It'll go up my nose.*

"Lewis," I tried to say. Instead of words, saliva dribbled from my mouth—*or was it blood?* "Woowis," I began again. *Damn. Now, I can't remember what I wanted to say.*

"I'm right here, Thea. Don't talk." Somewhere close by, the moan of a siren unraveled.

"Woowis!" I thought I shouted. With my head pressed to the cement, it was difficult for me to see out of my one exposed eye. He seemed to push himself off his knees with great effort.

"She tripped on the top step and fell all the way down." I heard his voice rasp. "I couldn't catch her."

"Okay, sir," said a uniformed giant. "Let us talk to her."

There were two of them—giants, I mean—dressed in black or something dark, like shadows.

"Woowis!"

He kneeled again to hear me. "Yes, Thea."

"Call Karen and Oda, in my book, purse." My mind wasn't clear enough to make decisions. "Kaiser card—wallet." I hoped he understood me. Once more darkness descended.

I came to with flickering shadows cocooning me. A hand the size of a ham touched my forehead. A deep voice said, "We're going to lift you onto the stretcher now. First, we need to straighten your leg then turn you over onto your back. This may hurt. Relax. Let us do the work."

Cranes of massive muscle hoisted me off the dirty carpet and freezing floor. The two in navy blue spoke. "On the count of three—ready—one, two, *three*," and I was flipped face up and slid onto a cloth-covered board.

I passed out. How long I was unconscious that time, I don't know, but finally I opened one eye, to see a smiling face with a sandy mustache, Western-style, leaning over me.

"Ma'am, you can let go of your purse now. We need to place straps across your arms and legs." He spoke slowly as though talking to a child.

I mumbled "Okay" through swollen lips.

Somebody touched my shoulder. "Can you straighten your leg?" He tugged at my right knee.

"No!" I screamed. But I heard no sound.

The business-like voice moved closer. "We didn't get that. Would you repeat?"

Shaking my head was just as painful as trying to speak.

He touched my right knee, pressing gently.

"No!" Ooohh—blackness, then pinpoints of stars. Trickles of perspiration accumulated at my hair line.

"Ready?" said both men together. A pillow was slipped under my knee.

Abruptly, I was shoved into the back of the ambulance. *Oh, my God. This is worse than having a baby or passing kidney stones.* "Wait! Woowith?"

"I'm right here, Thea. I'll follow the ambulance in my car." He looked drained of energy, his face pale.

"I'm thorry." Uncontrollable tears streamed from the corners of my eyes.

"I still have your tooth," he called after me as the paramedics belted me in and the siren wailed.

Tooth, what tooth?"

The ambulance stopped moving. The doors opened and the night air smacked me in the face. An angel stood on the ramp, the building's floodlights highlighting her blonde hair. *Dear Oda. I wonder how she got here so fast without a siren.* Jogging alongside the stretcher, she whispered, "Thea, can you wiggle your toes?"

"Yeth."

"Can you move your head?"

I nodded slightly before a migraine gripped my skull in a vise.

The stretcher stopped moving.

"Doesn't appear that your neck or back is broken," she whispered.

She stood by quietly while people in white fluttered around me.

"Karen?" Just as I said her name, my daughter appeared. Once again I wondered how she'd arrived so quickly.

Maybe I'd lost any sense of real time, fading in and out of consciousness.

After transferring me to a hospital bed, my knights in blue allowed the nurses to take over. "Thank you," I tried to say, but they were on their way to rescue another in distress.

"I'm putting your shoes and purse in this plastic bag," said a nurse, placing it on a nearby chair.

Whatever. If only they'd give me a pain killer and let me go home. I'm so cold.

Somehow, somewhere, Oda found a blanket to replace the one the paramedics took away with them. She very carefully tucked it around me. I began to relax with her comforting, gentle touch.

A woman wearing a long white coat and a stethoscope appeared at my bedside, clipboard in hand. Her red hair wound into a topknot added a bit of whimsy to her serious expression. "How do you feel?" she asked.

How do you think I feel?

"Can you get her out of her coat?" she asked the nurses.

The two nurses on either side of me eased my arms out of my denim duster with blood stains spattered down the front.

I couldn't hold back a groan.

"We're being as gentle as we can," said one of them, "but we have to remove this coat."

The doctor, her green eyes steady, said, "Mrs. Clark, you realize, don't you, that your front tooth has been snapped off?"

What? Oh, that's the tooth Lewis is talking about.

She glanced at Karen. "Call her dentist right away. You don't want infection in the exposed gum."

The doctor removed the blanket from my legs. "I don't see any blood on your legs or arms. But we'll know more after the X-rays." She patted my hand, and nodded curtly at the nurse holding a syringe.

Please, please, a pain-killer. I closed my eyes, at least the one eye that I could control. My shivering progressed into shaking. I noticed Karen glancing around the cubicle.

She asked, "Could she have another blanket? Her hands are really cold."

The nurse frowned but turned on her heel, then returned with a second blanket. She smiled sympathetically, offering it to Karen.

Holding one of my hands, Oda managed acupressure on my wrist before a technician arrived with another gurney. "Mr. Washington," his name tag announced. He and the painkiller nurse stood side by side on my left. I could feel their body densities.

Uh oh. They are conspiring something. I heard him say, "On the count of three." *Oh, that again.* And, they pulled my train-wrecked body onto another gurney.

Oh, dammit to hell. Shit, that hurt! When is that painkiller going to kick in?

I saw worry and concern on my daughter's face. Tears filled my eyes again. Most of my life I'd been the one comforting others. I tried to reassure her I was okay but, turning my head, however slightly, made me dizzy. My face must have contorted because Oda quickly placed her hands gently on either side of my skull. How wonderful the soothing heat felt emanating from her palms.

The ride to radiology seemed long and bumpy. "Sorry, I'm being as careful as I can," Mr. W. said.

When he flicked on the overhead fluorescent lights, I winced. *Ooh! So bright.* I wanted to shield my one eye from the intensity, but my arms weren't following my brain's directions.

Mr. W. parallel-parked the gurney. "Can you scoot onto the X-ray table by yourself?"

I wanted to laugh. I tried to look disgusted. *Doesn't anyone understand?* "No," I said, then very slowly and deliberately, "I fell down twenty-one damn theps."

"Okay, okay, Ma'am," he said quietly. "I have a possible solution, but you'll have to wait here while I look for a certain contraption. Don't move."

Don't move! Everyone's a comedian.

Mr. Washington returned with an apparatus that looked like an army cot with handles on four waist-high poles. *How the hell do I get on that? Will that thing hold me?* Compared to the solidity of the X–ray table, the canvas hammock looked precarious.

Lord, Don't let me fall again.

48

To Be In Shock, Or Not To Be

Karen and Oda followed the gurney to X-ray. *My daughter and my friend are take-charge people. I'm in good hands.*

Mr. W. said, "Mrs. Clark, I have to lift your body to get the sheet underneath you." He glanced at the two women. "Will you help keep her arms at her sides and steady her?" To me, "Now, Mrs. Clark, can you lift up your bottom a few inches?"

I stared at the hospital green ceiling to keep from screaming. *No, I can't lift my bottom.*

He went right on, "The four wheels are locked. This portable gurney will not move." He grunted with the effort of lifting me carefully over onto the canvas sling.

Shit! Even with three people working together to shift me, every place they touched screamed. I heard a breath explode and then a groan. *Oh me, oh my. Just let me die. Oooh, I'm floating away.*

"Mom! Stay with us."

Damnation! I knew Mr. W. tried to be gentle as he straightened my arms and legs but the pain reminded me of the medieval dungeons where they tortured people on the rack. He leaned close to me, "Now, I need you to turn over."

I swallowed with difficulty, the metallic taste of blood overpowering. I gasped, "I can't do it." *Can't he see my arms aren't working? And, dammit it to hell again, I've got to pee.*

Mr. W. was not to be deterred. "Once I do your back and legs that will be it and you can return to Emergency."

No time or place to be ladylike. I growled, "Help me get off." And before he could ask, I said, "No bed pan." I knew I didn't have the muscle power to settle my buns on another cold hard object. God help me—I wasn't going to embarrass myself by wetting the only clothes I had.

It took Oda, Karen, and Mr. W. to get me off the table and upright. *Why isn't that pain-killer working? What was in that syringe anyway? Water?*

Karen and Oda half carried me while I hobbled cross-legged the ten steps to the restroom with a Unisex sign on the door. I didn't care about its sex as long as it had a seat and toilet tissue. Hell! I didn't even care about the toilet tissue. Then, I agonized on the endless trip back to Marie Curie's invention—damn her. Why didn't she invent a crane to lift me up and over?

"What's wrong, Mom?"

"I'm falling off. Really dithy." With my one eye opened as far as I could, I noticed Oda and Karen sending a message to each other. Quickly they moved to book-end my head and to hold me steady while Mr. W. clicked the pictures needed.

At the door Mr. Washington said, "Sorry to keep you on the table. I'll be back after I get the photos to the doctor."

"Don't hurry," said Oda, and she began applying pressure on my legs below my knees.

Still at the door, Mr. W. asked, "What are you doing?"

"Just some acupressure for shock," she said calmly.

They stared at each other. "I know a little about acupressure," he said. "How long do you need?"

"Fifteen minutes to stop her shaking."

I could feel her warm hands moving on my legs. *Ooh, that feels good.*

When Mr. Washington returned, I was much calmer.

"The doctor is examining the X-rays," he said. "She wants you in Emergency to explain what she sees." He wheeled another gurney alongside the X-ray table.

Oh, dear. With all the upping and downing I might as well walk back. I didn't know if I'd broken anything but I could tell I'd squashed a lot of soft tissue. My back muscles felt like overdone pasta. I smiled at my own little joke.

Karen asked softly, "What's funny, Mom?"

I closed my eyes remembering Lewis's mantra: *"Keep your muscle tone. Lay your arms lightly on mine as you pull yourself upward into your best posture. No spaghetti arms."* When did he say that? My brain was mush.

The bumping down the hall ceased and I was back in my temporarily assigned cubicle. With my X-rays in her hands, the red-haired doctor waited until Karen and Oda were by my side.

"Mrs. Clark, you are very lucky."

Lucky! Lady Luck must be on the freeway to L.A. I don't feel lucky.

The doctor said, "I don't see anything but an old fracture in the coccyx area."

What old fracture? Oh, the Caribbean cruise, when I slipped doing the Twist with Michael and sat down hard on my tail bone. You really do see stars. The Caribbean's baby blue sky had turned black, eventually receding with pin-points of light.

The doctor's voice penetrated my fog. She was talking to Karen, handing her a sheaf of instructions. "You'll call her dentist tonight? I've made a note of the type of fracture that separated the tooth from the gum." The red-haired medic released the form from her clipboard. "Your mom has a mild concussion. I've written instructions for at-home care." She stared at Karen. "Now, if you have no more questions, I'll let the nurse wheel her out." And to me, "Home you go," and offering a perfunctory smile, moved on to her next patient.

That's it?

Karen, Oda and the nurse helped me into the chair. "I want my thoos, pleethe."

The nurse put the plastic bag containing my purse, coat and shoes in my lap.

"I mean, I want my thoos on." I was determined to wear my shoes but my feet or ankles must have swelled because Karen had a hard time pushing on each high heel. "Help me thtand."

"Mom, you're not walking. You have to be wheeled out to the car. That's hospital policy."

"I want to get up on my feet." I said as wind whistled though a hole in my uppers.

The nurse protested.

"I'm all right."

The tall thin nurse looked down at Karen. "Is she always this stubborn?"

Karen rolled her eyes heavenward. She leaned over and planted a light kiss on my forehead, the only piece of skin apparently not scraped or bleeding. She took the plastic bag containing my belongings and draped my old denim duster around my shoulders.

In the Emergency Room, Lewis and Christina sat close together clasping each other's hands. Lewis rose, hurried forward; Christina followed. My heart hurt when I saw how pale and drained they looked.

I smiled the best I could as Karen, Oda, and the nurse pulled me upward. The wall clock said ten fifteen. My gosh. They'd waited over four hours.

"Hi, Woowith." I stretched my swollen mouth another quarter of an inch. "Thee, I'm all right." Their shocked expressions said otherwise.

Christina and Lewis followed my chair as the nurse wheeled me to the doors leading to the parking lot.

Karen left my side to bring her car close to the ramp.

Of course, I hadn't seen a mirror. I didn't know I was a

twin to the Hunchback of Notre Dame. Landing on the right half of my face had pushed that side to the left. My face was no longer an oval but triangular; blood and perspiration matted my hair; caked blood outlined my mouth adding a ghoulish effect.

Lewis remained mute while he walked beside me.

"How many weekth till the comp, Woowis?"

"Three," he mumbled.

"With Oda'th help, I can be ready."

Nobody laughed.

Lewis dipped his head and lowered his voice. "Thea, tomorrow I'm calling the comp organizers to remove your name from the list of competitors and refund your money."

"First, the dentist," interrupted Karen. "I'll leave a message with Dr. Solomon's service."

I swallowed to create some spit. "Woowis, can you drive me to dentitht tomorrow?" I wanted someone strong in case I slipped or fainted.

"I'll be at your house whenever you say and stay with you as long as you need me."

With Oda's help, he tucked me into the front seat.

Ever so gently touching the tip of my nose, he said, "I'm so sorry. I'm really so sorry." I knew Lewis wanted to give me a reassuring hug, but he held back. He and Christina waved goodbye; I watched them slowly walk to their car.

"Oda," I heard Karen say, "I'll drive ahead. Have the garage door and the patio door open so we can bring Mom in through the kitchen."

Living a mile and a half from the hospital was an advantage this day. Six minutes later, Oda pulled into my garage, honking the horn. Karen appeared and soon all three of us were groaning and sweating with effort to move me inside to the dining area.

We rested, me panting, standing up, holding onto the wrought iron table.

Karen touched my shoulder gently. "Mom, how can we make it easier for you? And how can we get you upstairs?" She pointed toward the living room sofa. "Or would you rather sleep on the couch?"

I shook my head rattling the marbles.

"Karen," said Oda. "I'll pull, you push from behind."

God. Somebody. Help! Just let me melt here like the Wicked Witch of the West.

"C'mon, Thea," said Oda, "you can do it. Remember the Lao Tse saying, 'A Journey of thousand steps begins with a single step'."

Not funny. An hour later, it seemed, I was only partway up Mt. Fujii.

"We're halfway," said Oda. "Help yourself a little bit. Karen and I are doing our best. And where is that Luke when you need him?"

I rolled my one eye. Finally, I was at the top of the stairs and limped down the hallway to my bedroom. It took the two of them to undress me and slip on a nightgown. Pride and modesty were overridden by need of the moment. With a warm shawl now around my neck and shoulders, I sat propped against my oversize pillow.

Oda placed several needles in both legs below the knees. "I can't put them in your face just yet. I need to hear what your dentist says."

Suddenly, in the doorway stood my granddaughter, Jolene. "I'm going to stay with you and Mom tonight." In her arms she held a sleeping bag.

"Jolene," said Karen. "You can put that on the floor next to Grandma. Tonight, be aware of how Grandma sleeps. See that she doesn't roll over on her face. And this is really important. Listen for any irregular breathing. The doctor said she has a concussion. We need to watch her closely for the next twenty-four hours."

Oda stood at the foot of my bed. "Karen," she said. "Did you notice Mr. W. taking head X-rays?"

Karen shook her head.

"Seems those should have been ordered." She was silent, then, "Karen, would you warm some hand towels to wrap around her legs? After I remove the needles, we need to keep her legs warm till she goes to sleep."

In my walk-in closet Karen found two heating pads, plugged them in, gently pushing one in between the handmade over-sized pillow and my back.

After insertion of the super-fine needles in my legs, Oda heated their heads with a moxibustion wand.

The herbal fragrances emanating from the cigar-shaped wand soothed me. "Thank you."

"I'm going to attach an electrical Tens unit to some of the needles. You'll hardly feel the vibration but that will help relieve pain also. And now, Karen, how about a cup of tea for the three of us, you, Jolene and me?"

"Good idea."

Soon, very drowsy with drugs and the calming effect of acupuncture and warmth, I barely remembered Oda saying goodbye.

"I'll be back tomorrow after work." And she left for her own condominium across the street.

Putting aside the tea things, Jolene asked, "Would you like me to wash your face and brush your teeth, Grandma?"

I made a negative motion with my hand. *Nothing, not no one touches my mouth. Thank goodness, the pain killer is dulling the agony.*

I dozed sitting up. Subconsciously, I knew tomorrow was going to be a bitch.

49

Toof? What Toof?

As late as it was, Dr. Solomon returned Karen's call. "Have Thea at my office at 8:30 tomorrow. Bring along her X-rays."

Next, Karen called Lewis, apologizing for the hour. "I'll be at your house at seven-thirty," he said. "Don't worry about disturbing me. I can't sleep."

"That truly must have been awful for you," Karen said.

Lewis went on, "We've cancelled classes and appointments of the students we could reach. The others, Christina will teach in my place."

The next morning Jolene woke me at half past six to help me dress for the twenty-mile trip to the dentist. "Grandma," she said after answering the bedroom phone, "It's Lewis, checking to make sure you'll be ready by the time he gets here. And, don't talk. Nod yes or no or even move your eyelid, I'll catch on."

Can't talk; can't move. Oh me, oh my. Can I walk? Hell! How am I going to get off the bed? How am I going to get downstairs? I just want to stay here.

"Grandma, time to get up. I have your clothes."

Perspiring, Jolene finally had me dressed in slacks, worn slip-on sandals and a zip up sweater. Forget the bra. "Enough clothes to make you decent," she said. "I'll go downstairs and heat some herbal tea for you. Can you stay on the edge of the bed?"

Another comedian. "No thee, thank you." Tears flowed for all the babies born with cleft lips. That's exactly what my mouth felt like.

"Luke!" I heard Jolene call down the hall. "Need you. Get dressed."

With Luke in front and Jolene behind, holding my waistband, I crept downstairs one step at a time. At the bottom, I held tight to the wrought iron railing, my breathing noisy and labored.

"Grandma, I wish we had a wheel chair," said Jolene.

"Thokay. I can walk."

She had already opened the garage door for Lewis and shortly we heard his car. He strode into the kitchen, anxiety sculpted on his face. When he saw me, he stopped abruptly. He tried to disguise his shock, but his face and body language betrayed my appearance better than any mirror. "Where can I touch her?"

Jolene shrugged.

"Jolene," Luke said. "I'll take over. Grandma, I'm putting my arms under your armpits and I'm going to half carry you to the garage. I know this will hurt. I'll get you there quickly as I can." At the car Luke held my arms steady as Lewis helped me sit. Shifting my legs inside the car hurt more than anything I'd ever experienced, including childbirth.

No! Your Other Left Foot

This truly feels like being drawn through a jagged knothole. Why don't they just sock me in the jaw. Put me out of my misery.

Two freeways and endless stoplights later, Lewis parked at the rear entrance of the dentists' suites in the medical complex, a few feet from the back door. He pressed the door bell.

Jenny, the hygienist, opened the back door and gently took my elbow to help Lewis extricate me from the front seat. Inside, she guided me into a patient chair and cautiously fastened a bib. She said nothing as she poured water into a paper cup, placing it within my reach. Her eyes were liquid; she washed my aura with her sympathy.

Lewis and Dr. Solomon on either side helped me lean back into the headpiece.

"Okay," said Dr. Phil, "may I have the X-rays?" Opening the oversized envelope, he said, "Where are the skull pics?" His blue eyes spit sparks and his eyebrows arched. "You didn't bring head X-rays?"

Lewis looked puzzled. "We brought the envelope they gave Thea."

Dr. Solomon said to Lewis, "She fell on her head and the hospital didn't take X-rays of her skull?" The doctor, our neighbor and close friend for years, clearly did not like what he saw when he stared down at me.

"Juth back and legs," I muttered, growing increasingly anxious about the wind whistling through my teeth. Anger fed my anxiety. What was that emergency doctor thinking? Didn't anyone foresee this problem? Oh, God. Not the X-ray table again! Should I have said something about my face at the hospital? *Aren't they supposed to take care of me? Even when you are practically unconscious, must you be your own advocate?*

The doctor shook his head. His shoulders sagged. "Thea, I'm sorry you made the difficult trip over here. I can't work on your mouth before checking the pictures." He turned to Lewis. "She might have multiple face fractures. See this deep vertical crease in her eyebrow. That also might indicate a problem. Jenny, get me the hospital X-ray lab on the phone."

The hygienist had been so still, I forgot she was in the room. She turned on her heel, spoke some unintelligible words into the hall phone, then handed the receiver to the doctor.

"Thank you," he said. He touched my shoulder gently. "After I make this call, I'll be right back. Try to relax." His determined departure left a wake of unspent fury.

Dr. Solomon's words echoed in the hall. "I'm returning for X-rays my patient who fell down stairs last night. Legs and back X-rayed but not her skull." He paused to listen then cut in, "She has a severely damaged face. I can't understand why cranial views weren't ordered. I'm sending her back to you. She will be there in an hour. I want her given priority." In a quieter voice he said, "Thank you."

I was comforted by his repressed disgust. *Action coming up—ta da!*

The next two hours were a traumatic haze. In and out of Lewis's car. In and out of the hospital. On and off the X-ray table. This time it took two of them to hoist me onto the table in a "flying nun" position with my head face down in a hole for a three-dimensional X-ray. Then, I was stood up against another machine for side views.

By noon we'd returned to Dr. Solomon's. After reading the X-rays, he said, "Amazing. No facial fractures, the only break is at the gum where the tooth was snapped off." He stood still for a few moments. Then, gently he said, "Open your mouth as much as you can. It will hurt, I know, but I'll help you." With both hands he cupped my jaw. "Thea, I have to touch your mouth and gum. I'll be quick when you open wide. I'm going to attach a dental strip to your upper teeth. This will be attached to either side of the gap. I can't do more than that just now."

He nodded at Jenny to move closer with the tray of implements.

Lightly he touched my arm saying, "This will feel weird, but it will help keep food, liquids and air away from the exposed nerves."

He saw me flinch; he glanced at Lewis. "Didn't they give her any medication for pain?"

"She has pills with her but wouldn't take any because the water hurt," he said.

"So, she hasn't eaten anything either?"

Lewis again shook his head.

"Thea," said Dr. Solomon, "Jenny'll warm some water. Take the pills."

"Good," he said, after I'd swallowed two tablets. He

shook his finger at me. "You are very very lucky,"

There it is again—luck. What is it with doctors?

"I want to wait until more of the swelling goes down before I begin work on a new tooth," he said. "Can you cope with that strip of adhesive in your mouth for a week?"

I blinked yes.

"Now, go home, eat, rest."

To distract myself from the searing pain of lowering myself onto the car's seat, I focused on Lewis's face. His anguished expression spoke eloquently of his own torture. Once more, my eyes filled.

The salt in a tear stung my damaged cheek.

"Thea," he said turning the key in the ignition. "I really did try to grab hold of your coat. I reached for your coat, but couldn't hold on."

I slowly stretched my hand to gently touch his on the steering wheel.

On the way back to San Pedro, Lewis suggested we stop for food.

I offered my mini-nod.

Being past noon, I was sure he was hungry. He drove into a Spires parking lot. "You need something in your stomach—at least warm liquid." As the eldest in a large family, he was used to taking charge. He parked as close to the restaurant's front door as he could.

Our waitress tried not to stare as she led us to a rear booth. The pain pills I'd taken at Dr. Solomon's began to work.

Seated customers glanced away when I limped by them.

Lewis ordered beef broth with an ice cube on the side, a glass of lukewarm water, a straw, and then a roast beef sandwich for himself.

When he finished eating he said, "I'm going to use the pay phone over there to let Jolene know we'll be at your garage in twenty minutes."

I fluttered an eyelid.

We rode in silence toward San Pedro. Even in the restaurant we'd been wordless. Now, at my house again I faced the Himalayas, the stairs to the second floor. Lewis wanted to carry me up and have the expedition over with, but there was no place on my body he could take hold without my cringing.

Jolene met us in the garage and led the way upstairs. She had pulled aside the bed covers and plumped up the huge pillow. Gently, Lewis helped me sit on the edge of the mattress, while she removed my sandals.

Rising, she said to him, "I can take over."

"Call me when you need anything," he said. "I can be here in five minutes. I'll let myself out." Then he sent me a sweet smile, his eyes sad.

I gave him a thumbs up but he'd disappeared down the hall. My energy was dissipating fast. I still hadn't seen myself.

"Jolene, a mirror, pleath."

"Grandma." Her questioning eyes met mine. "Maybe tomorrow?" Interpreting my stubborn look, she shrugged. "Is this the one you want?" She held up a double-sided mirror.

Gingerly, she sat beside me and held up the mirror with reluctance. No wonder people stared.

How grotesque. Oops! That's the magnifying side! Even when I turned over the mirror, the right side of my face appeared twice as large as the other. I was one large triangular puff pastry. I beheld the face of an aged prize fighter who had lost his last fight.

"Thea," my dentist had said, "don't tongue the strip's edges and accidentally loosen it."

I know, I know. That will be hard not to do. Hard? Impossible. Gosh. George Washington with his wood and ivory teeth popped into my head. *What a pain for him.*

Jolene moved a straight chair against the wash basin cabinet so that, in a seated position, I could lean my elbows on the counter to wash my face. "Jolene, hand me thom cotton ball. I turned on the hot water, using warm liquid only, and dabbed at my face. Next, to brush my teeth." *Oh, Fudgecicles. Forget the teeth!*

Bless my granddaughter! She never complained about the twenty-four hour duty. And six days after I'd fallen, she cooked Christmas dinner for fourteen family members. Two days before, with her best friend, Lana, they had gift-wrapped the presents I'd bought and hidden in my bedroom closet.

Jolene also knew where I stored Christmas decorations in the garage. "Grandma, would you like Lana and me to bring in the tree from the patio? We've been watering it all week."

She waited. "Would you like us to set it up?"

My swollen cheeks did their best to create a smile.

"That's a yes?"

Later, the girls told me how they stood the tree in its annual corner and filled its branches with memories in the shapes of ornaments commemorating years of family history.

Suddenly, I heard Jolene exclaim, "Here's the little snow girl with my name on it that Nana bought when I was born." I heard silence. Then, "This is the third year she's not been here for Christmas. I miss her."

Sounds of vacuuming whirled up the stairs. Jolene and Lana giggled their way into my room. "We dusted and arranged your miniature nativity scene on the antique card table. We hope you'll like it. And, that grubby old Santa doll that Momma looks for every year is now under the tree."

I wanted to laugh but could only make a gurgling sound.

The day before Christmas, Karen dropped off the groceries for the next day's dinner. That morning the kitchen underneath my bedroom reverberated with laughter as supplies and tasks were organized. Suddenly, I heard a sweet lyrical sound. Jolene and her mother were harmonizing on "Joy to the World." I closed my eyes and eased my muscles, slowly, carefully stretching. Waves of happy notes wafted throughout the house, blanketing me with tender tones.

I'd discovered that taking in air through my nose hurt less than breathing through my mouth. Pulling in and holding a long sniff, I captured the smells of a vegetable casserole, particularly the aroma of onions. That day the most expensive perfume in the world couldn't compare with that vegetable bouquet.

Later in the morning, Karen called my son and his wife. "Remind the children Mom looks awful—but don't scare them. Don't hug her either."

Christmas Day, Luke installed me in the rose velvet wing chair facing the front door. I wore dark glasses because my eyes were still black and blue and swollen.

Shortly before, Jolene and Luke helped me rappel back down my Himalayas. Terrified that I'd slip over the edge of a stair, I held onto Jolene, probably leaving fingernail marks on her shoulders.

My son and his family arrived first, everyone carrying as many colorful bundles as they could. I ached when I saw the young children edge slowly toward me as though any breeze they'd stir up might blow me over.

Six-year-old Tyler lightly touched my knee. My heart melted. Halley, at eight, ever the keen observer, asked, "Why are you wearing dark glasses in the house, Grandma? And did you get your ears pierced? What are those gold balls?"

I smiled the best I could and looked at Jolene. "Those are acupuncture studs in her ears," Jolene said. "Helps ease the pain."

My appearance acted as a reminder of how fragile life can be. The adults, tense with watchfulness, insisted on a quieter celebration.

Of the delicious and fragrant dinner, I ate only the mashed potatoes drowned in gravy and a couple of spoonfuls of jellied cranberry sauce. At the table, I looked longingly at the drumsticks, the dark meat being my favorite. *Not able to chew, maybe I'll lose fat I don't need. Always a silver lining.*

As dinner neared an end, some signal passed between Nancy and Karen. Perhaps they saw strain making more furrows in my brow. "Let's have our pie in the living room," said Karen.

"Children," Nancy said, "help clear the table."

Luke helped me back into my comfortable wing chair. Karen and Nancy organized what they thought would be quiet games with the younger children.

Before dark, our celebration drew to a close. Parents packed up gifts and children carried what they could to their own cars. Luke and Jolene pushed and pulled exhausted me back up the stairs.

Later, sitting up in bed, tears gently trickled down my lopsided face. *Thank you, God, for my loving family. I'm truly grateful to be alive*

50

Back to Work Too Soon

THE NEXT WEEK it took me a half hour to get down the stairs on my own. In the kitchen, I'd made a cup of tea and settled in front of the TV for the news when I heard the sound of a key turning in the front door lock. Only family members had a key so I didn't move.

"Hi, Grandma." Jolene dropped her backpack by the front door. "How're you feeling today?"

"Better." I clicked off the TV and smiled at my oldest grandchild, now a high school senior.

She kissed me lightly on my forehead. "You're looking pretty good for . . ." She searched for the right word.

I made a face using muscles that still protested and shrugged. "Soon I'll need to go back to work. And let you return to your normal schedule."

She touched my hand. "I like coming by after school. It's only been two weeks. Besides, Mom depends on my report. Now I'm going to make you a light supper then I'll call Dad to pick me up." She bustled around the kitchen, talking all the while about her day at school.

The next Monday, against family advice, I limped into my office at the retirement home. I lasted two hours. The residents and the staff stared at me with horrified sympathy. "Go home," said David B. the manager. "Barbara and I will take over your afternoon program."

What wonderful people I work with. But what am I going to do if I can't work? And right now, I certainly can't dance. Just what is my future?

While days were painfully exhausting, nights were worse. The vertigo almost defeated me. After falling off a horse at full gallop in my teens, I knew all about being off-balance. But on waking in shadowy darkness with the furniture and walls rocking side to side, I felt really drunk and hung over. I was terrified this would last forever.

Karen asked one evening, "Mom, is it all right with you if we rearrange your bedroom a bit?"

"Like what?"

"Like moving these small chests of drawers on either side of your bed so when you awake in the dark, you can reach out to touch them."

"Good idea." And it worked. I was grateful. Even so, every morning, I still had the mother of all hangovers.

51

Twenty-One Steps Revisited

OF COURSE, I DID NOT COMPETE at San Diego in three weeks. My face was still triangular and jaundiced—beautiful I was not. Inertia and depression marbled my days. I needed to confront my fear about my future. It had been a month since the fall, when in a trembling voice I called Lewis for an appointment.

"Are you sure you're ready?"

"You know the old cliché about falling off a horse."

He didn't laugh.

Backing my car out of the garage was a still a struggle. When I twisted to look over my shoulder, I'd feel a tearing. My back screamed, "Don't do that." True to the old cliché: Fish or cut bait, it was either dance or quit. One day, I drove to the dance studio, parked the car as close as I could to the entrance, then sat staring through the glass door at those fateful stairs. Could I face the twenty-one steps with damaged muscle memory and the awful mildewy smell of the fake grass still fresh in my nose?

Just do it, Thea.

I dragged myself out of the car and began the short trek across the pot-holed tarmac. In the fading light of the late afternoon, I dared not look down to see where I walked because of my vertigo. I might have used Nana's cane that I now kept in the car. But how would that look, limping into a dance studio leaning on a three-pronged metal walking stick?

Thank goodness! Here's the door. My hand reached for the handle, but hesitated just as it had that very first lesson with Michael two years before. Experiencing similar apprehension, even a premonition that something momentous was about to happen, I stood awash in my feelings about Michael.

You can still turn around and go home. Oh, don't be a such a wuss. Open the damn door for God's sake. Carrying my dance bag over one arm and holding ajar the heavy glass door, I hopped inside before the door slapped my behind. I didn't see any dried blood on the old green carpet. *Well, it's been a month. Wait. There is no old green carpet. It's blue, flat and new. Take hold of the shiny railing. Shiny railing? That's new, too. Hmmm. There's the first step. Deep breath.*

I'd been anxiously navigating the stairs at home several times a day. Suddenly, muscle memory paralyzed me, kinesthetic images of my body rolling over and over and, slamming against the side walls on the fast track to the bottom. My legs trembled; the dance bag felt like a canvas bag of bricks, my still-tender mouth winced with every deep intake of air. *How can I dance if I can't breathe?* Tears of frustration blurred my vision. But I'm stubborn. I pulled myself upward.

Bless him, Lewis stood at the top. He must have heard my grunting.

"Hi." He started down. "I'm coming."

"No. I'm getting there—slowly." *Very slowly.* "I'm okay," I called up. I was doing the actual work but what I saw of his body language said he was right beside me, mentally pulling and pushing.

Finally, I reached the landing, catching my breath, gripping the railing, afraid to turn to see where I'd been.

Lewis took my elbow, pulling me forward, gently releasing my dance bag from my clammy hand. I smiled a thank you, knowing my liver yellow face was still off-center.

That's interesting, new carpet here too. Where's that loose thread? Gone. Ooh, how lovely that ugly beige couch looks! There it sat homesteading its usual place. I wanted to hug it. Instead, I painfully straightened my back, sucked in my stomach muscles and with Lewis's help, I lowered myself on the old saggy cushions.

Several couples glided by and smiled.

I felt my face crease in a goofy grin. *I'm home.*

When the waltz music stopped, a tall lithe brunette left her partner to sit next to me. "Aren't you the woman who fell down the steps just before Christmas?"

I shrugged in a deprecating gesture.

"That was terrible. Until you began to move, we thought you were dead. It was pretty dramatic here after the paramedics took you away." She grimaced. "Dancers are a superstitious lot. A bad fall is our worst nightmare."

"I only lost a tooth." Downplaying the event, I smiled and said, "See?"

She pretended to look. "I don't mean to insult you. You're older than most amateurs here, aren't you? But I do often see you practicing. Maybe that's why you didn't do more damage, break an arm, or a leg, or even, heaven forbid, your back."

Lewis entered the conversation. Lightly touching my knee he said, "Do you really want to try dancing today?"

Extricating my shoes from their bag, I smiled.

"Here," he held out his hand. "Let me put those on for you."

The tall brunette rejoined her partner on the floor for a foxtrot.

"Bending down still gives me a headache. Thank you." With my shoes buckled, I placed my hands on Lewis's shoulders to push myself upward.

"Well done," he said, rising to his full height. He cupped my elbow gently, escorting me from the alcove onto the polished hardwood floor. "Let's try a slow rumba first. Don't listen to the music. We'll dance in the center letting the others move around us. They'll give us space. I'll be careful we aren't bumped."

I shivered, fearing collisions I knew he wouldn't allow. We took Latin dance position and began Cuban motion. *Ow! My hips don't want to gyrate like that, not just yet.* I knew that traditionally, dancers move counter-clockwise, in line-of-dance. But rumba being a "spot" dance, we stayed in the middle. The others circled around us like spokes of a wheel with us the hub. But within five minutes, I was winded.

"We can sit down if you like." Lewis squeezed my hand.

"No. The more I move, the more I can. But, oh, my...."

"What is it, Thea?"

"I'm so dizzy."

"I've got you. Hey, remember what I've always told you. Don't look down. Look up, over my right shoulder, past my ear at the ceiling. I won't let you fall."

"I know you won't." Tears spilled over. "Falling is what I do." I tried to laugh.

He stopped moving and gave me a hug. "Ooh! Thea, Thea, Thea."

Twenty minutes later and I was finished, literally.

I noticed Lewis observing me closely. "Go on. Tell me about being unsteady."

"Even sitting like this, when I move my head sharply sideways, I get dizzy. I'm constantly aware that I might lose my balance. I never worried about falling before my accident."

He gazed at me with those expressive eyes. "You did great today," he said, "but don't push yourself." He shrugged. "I know, it's useless to say that."

"Are you cross with me?"

"Oh, no. Just worried about you. I've relived your fall so many times. I still have nightmares."

So consumed with my own pain, I hadn't thought about the full impact on Lewis. To me, not dancing would mean losing my connection with him. I'd feel bereft. I'd felt part of his extended family. God! I'd miss that! I realized then, that he'd felt guilty and, because he really cared about me, he would hurt too in ways I might understand.

Kneeling on the floor, he unbuckled my shoes and slipped on my sandals. "When you're up to it, we'll go down the stairs together, but I'll go in front. Remember, I always lead." He signaled to Christina, who excused herself from her student and glided over to us. Lewis said, "I'm walking Thea to her car. Be right back." And to me, "Please call me when you get home."

I could see through the glass door at the bottom of the stairs. It was quite dark outside. With Lewis one step ahead of me, I inched down the stairs.

"Watch out for the potholes," he reminded me.

At my car door, I stopped to face him. "I know you tried to help me that day. It all happened so fast."

He pulled a face. "You tumbled over and over. All I could do was watch helplessly." He looked so dejected I put my arms around his waist and laid my head against his chest. There we stood in the dark for several seconds. *This is another kind of love. Thank you, God.*

On my way home, I wondered, how did I escape major injury? What saved me? I've always believed in angels. Maybe angel wings softened my fall. And then again, maybe this was one particular angel with golden-brown eyes, extra long lashes, and a smile that wrapped you up in a hug.

52

My Next Challenge

My obsession with dance obliterated doubts about my readiness to resume lessons. After four months of acupuncture and physical therapy, I felt my confidence return. One afternoon at the studio I said, "Lewis, I think I'm ready to compete." But my voice was a whisper and my heart beat rapidly.

"You're sure?"

"I want to challenge myself again."

We sat on that sagging couch still bookended by those two fifty gallon aquariums with their salt water fish ballets. He touched my hand. "The Orange County studio is preparing for its annual show. How about dancing one solo with me?"

"A showcase?"

"No. Not an in-studio show. A performance for a paying audience in a community auditorium."

"No judges?"

"No."

I'd gained twenty pounds since my last competition and I knew I couldn't get into my usual costumes. "I'd have to have a new dress."

He shrugged. "Your costume will depend on which dance you choose. Heck, I've seen you dance with stage fright and arthritis. I know that what you want to do, you will do."

I sat back against the lumpy pillows and reflected. In the past I'd entered competitions with confidence, even bravado. I'd been less experienced and more naive. Could I do what I knew was required? My vertigo, while no longer debilitating, had not disappeared. I had to be especially alert when descending stairs, even three or four at a time. "When is this show? And where?"

"Three months from now," he said. "Fullerton College auditorium."

A show, not a competition, not the same kind of pressure. I could have fun. I would invite my writing class. I fantasized, now they'll see what I'm writing about. They would see why I felt so passionate about dancing.

I'll do a knockout performance.

53

Stubbornness, Thy Name is Thea

SEVERAL WEEKS HAD PASSED, during which Wendy Johnson, international champion, choreographer and judge, designed a tango for me to music from Baz Luhrman's Moulin Rouge. The gut-grinding music of "Roxanne" and the Argentine tango made my chakras glow, especially affecting the orange and red levels. I felt excited by the earthy intensity of the pulsating beat. Wendy's choreography with its fans, kicks, and dips was tight and specific. Every step fit the next as in a puzzle. *Mistakes are out of the question.* In the past when I goofed, I trusted Lewis to cover up my error. Even in a non-judged performance, I could never stop and ask the stage manager to start the music over.

Almost healed from my injuries, for this event I'd practiced at a studio Lewis used in Santa Ana, about eighty miles away. I wasn't comfortable there; I felt like an outsider; I didn't know anyone to talk to. It was an older studio with a reputation carrying much prestige. I felt clumsy and old.

At this stage in my amateur career, I wanted to raise my own level to a spectacular performance. This could be the last time I ever danced in a show. Sadly, after my devastating fall, I realized this could be my "swan song."

Up to now, Lewis designed and sewed my costumes. To help me save money, he suggested I check out ready-mades. I'd long since spent my inheritance.

I bought a black silk jersey and chiffon skirt of overlapping panels. When I turned quickly, the panels flung themselves outward as if lifted by the blades of a fan. Next came a bustier and a black satin corset, that article of Victorian torture. Think Vivien Leigh in *Gone with the Wind* when she clutches the bed post as Hattie McDaniel pulls tight her corset's laces. My sexy black net and suede boots I'd ordered from a catalog. Breathlessly, I'd waited for their arrival. Thank God they fit perfectly when I tried them on the day before the performance.

To top off the costume, I had a huge fall of Shirley Temple curls, bright red in hue, attached to the crown of my head by a Spanish mantilla comb. A black beauty dot on my cheek and a red satin choker completed the French can-can ensemble.

The one-time only performance was scheduled for seven-thirty p.m. with a full dress rehearsal that day at one p.m. Signs in the Fullerton parking lot directed me to the auditorium and then to the women's dressing room. Even with twenty or so female bodies sardined in various stages of undress, the rectangular room was freezing. I'd prearranged an appointment with a professional makeup artist and sat on a rickety folding chair for a half an hour while she applied makeup and fake eyelashes.

Completely costumed, but not knowing what to do with myself, I looked for Lewis. To keep warm I wore a long coat over my costume and cotton gloves I found in a pocket. The one-time-only dress rehearsal was still an hour away. Lewis found me shivering just outside the dressing room.

"Your hands are freezing. Don't be so nervous, Thea. You know the steps well. We've practiced a lot."

His words neither relaxed nor comforted me. For some reason this time, I was terrified I'd make a mistake he couldn't fix. He also warned me about the brightness of the spotlight. And he'd especially admonished me, saying the dress rehearsal was it, no repeat rehearsal. No second chance.

Finally, the call to go backstage bounced off the walls of the sub-zero dressing room. Four women rushed out to join their partners and line up ahead of us.

I'd not remembered that stage fright had a smell, tangy as in perspiration, overlaid with perfumed cosmetics and foot powder. I stamped my feet to keep warm while each couple danced their solo, whether a waltz, swing, foxtrot, or a polka. Then I heard the first notes of my own music and Lewis hustled me onto the stage, darkened in between each performance. When the spotlight was turned on me full force, I froze. *This is torture.* "I can't do this, Lewis."

"Just start," he said. "Move your left leg then your right."

"I can't see anything." I felt I'd stepped in a deep dark hole. My vertigo returned with a vengeance. Without warning, in total panic, I broke away and escaped to the wings and daylight with Lewis striding after me. When he caught up to me, I turned to face him. *Thea, calm down.* "Okay, okay," I said, "let's start over. I'm sorry, Lewis, I didn't understand how really blinding the spot would be."

"I'm sorry, too. That's it. We've lost our place. They've moved on."

"You mean, we forfeit?" I could see how disappointed he was. I'd never let him down before. "Lewis, I'll ask Wendy, I'll beg her to let us have a second chance."

He shook his head. "This is the one and only dress rehearsal." He glared at me. "You don't get it."

Regardless, I picked my way across cables, and in and around a maze of curtains looking for Wendy, the show's director. When I found her, I said, "Please, please, let me try again. I do want to be in the show tonight."

When I heard her call up to the projection booth, she became my all-time favorite coach. "Hey, guys," she yelled. "There's one more to spot, then you're through until seven-thirty." Lewis cued our music again and we hurried onto center stage.

I performed the tango without error. I was limp with relief. *Can I do it all again for real later this evening?* Now only three p.m. and I'd been strapped in that damn bustier and high-heeled dance boots for four hours. I was weary, hungry, cold, and I needed to pee.

Lewis hugged me. "Go somewhere and relax, Thea. You'll be fine."

My family was to arrive just before the evening performance. I wished I hadn't invited my writing class after all. In my fantasy I'd been spectacular and the members would be impressed. But now I was filled with anxiety. I looked for a warm place to sit and took three of my Chinese herb tranquilizers.

In past shows, I found it fun to observe the chaos of backstage activity. This time, the muted movements of performers and stage hands unnerved me. When it was time to line up, I stumbled. *What is wrong with me?*

Lewis reached for my hand. "Careful, watch your step."

The couple on the program ahead of us strode to center stage and began a Viennese waltz. Three minutes later, they bowed to the audience as the latter clapped and yelled their names. Lewis squeezed my shoulders. "Our turn."

I'd waited hours for this moment.

The emcee announced our solo; the tango's throb began.

My heart filled my throat.

Lewis whispered, "Keep your eyes partially closed. Do not look directly at the spotlight. And trust me."

In the dark we walked to the fluorescent floor strips marking our place center stage and took skaters' side by side position. The spotlight found me and coated me with heat. Lewis held my hand firmly in his as I executed the opening forward kick followed by a fan step. Time felt gelatinous. I followed his commands but it took all my strength to ignore the bright light and stay focused.

My performance, in my own mind, had been a disaster, no passion, no grace, no joy, no pizzazz. I'd so concentrated on the correctness of the choreography that I'd washed out its character. The audience saw a cardboard version of the story of heartbreak and defiance I'd wanted to tell. I felt near fainting till suddenly the music and Lewis stopped.

Is it finally over?

"Bow," he said, patting me on the back, "I knew you'd come through."

"I'm glad I got through without mistakes. But I felt ill."

"You did fine."

He seemed to think my performance had been perfectly all right.

I thought it was crap. Running away from him, gesturing tearfully that I didn't want him to follow, I hurried to the dressing room to shed that damn corset.

"Thea," he called, "there's a cast party back at the studio. You know how to get there from here?"

"Thanks, Lewis, but I'm through. I'm going home."

"You sure? All performers are welcome, you know."

I smiled a pretend happiness.

"Is something wrong?"

I waved dismissingly and closed the dressing room door. Taking only seconds to don my street clothes, I tossed my costume and shoes into their bags then rushed from that icy dressing room to meet my family in the lobby. I wanted to thank them for coming to root for me, if nothing else.

"Mother," said Karen as everyone gathered around me, "you were dressed like a Victorian hooker. What were you thinking?"

The others murmured congratulations and gave me hugs.

What was I thinking? Why did I feel as though I'd made a fool of myself? When I'd first heard the tango music in the movie, Moulin Rouge, again those chakras vibrated. Could they have led me astray?

For a couple of years now I'd danced well, but I still played it safe, not dancing in any way I considered radical, but the pulsating intensity of this tango, the grinding and squealing of the musical instruments expressed sounds I wanted to be able to release. And Wendy knew I yearned to do a sexy dance. I wanted the performance to be perfect, yet I wanted to have fun. But my performance made me sick like I never expected.

Every summer I held a pool party at my condominium complex for the family's summer birthdays, inviting twenty or so people. A week after the show, I was so emotionally exhausted that I called my son and daughter-in-law and said I wasn't up to having the event. They heard something in my voice that indicated to them I needed help and they arrived at my place the next afternoon.

"Thea," said Nancy, " I'm packing a few of your things and we are going to take you to our place for a rest. We'll figure out the birthday celebration later."

I stayed cocooned in their master bedroom for ten days, barely eating or talking. I'd embarrassed myself in front of family and friends. And for the first time, I hadn't enjoyed dancing with Lewis. It was a terrible revelation and I couldn't tell him. Now, I really was depressed. *But, Thea, you know well that depression is just anger turned inwards. Acknowledge it; move on.*

So one morning I said, "Nancy, I need to go home and see my cats. My neighbor can't feed them forever." I knew Rusty and Fred would be glad to see me.

At least I lost those damnable twenty pounds

54

Lewis Pulls Me Through Again

Now I could fit into my handmade costumes. *Again all dressed up and nowhere to go.*

Serendipity. Home again. The phone rang. It was Lewis. "I haven't seen you for three weeks. Are you all right?"

"Sure," I said. "A bit thinner." *Ha ha twenty pounds.*

"I wanted to tell you how you amaze me. You danced perfectly at Fullerton."

"No, I didn't."

"I have a video that says differently."

"I don't want to see it." Seconds later, I said, "Shall I come in next week at my usual time?" Those missing twenty pounds showed that almost every alto cumulus cloud has a silver lining. I'd spent enough time feeling sorry for myself.

"Sure. And I want to tell you about an upcoming competition."

"Yes?"

"USBC in Florida."

Damn. Since I began lessons, I'd heard about this prestigious competition, the largest competition in the United States.

"Are you dancing?" I asked.

"Yes. I'm taking four students with me."

Pulse racing, I said, "Let's talk about it when I come in for my lesson." I hung up in slow-motion happiness.

My teacher friend, Ruth, when I told her I'd always wanted to go, said, "Go, Thea. Take your Dramamine, pack a book—do you have *Fear of Flying*?—go to Florida. Collect memories for your old age. Maybe someday you'll write your memoirs."

55

Florida

FROM THE AIR, hotel row in Miami is impressive. A long thin finger of land with uneven vertical stacks of high rises, bordered by a dazzling zinc-white beach on the Atlantic Ocean side and by a pristine canal harboring luxury yachts on the other. The Fountainbleu Hilton, the only curved building on the aerial view postcards, is known as the venue for championship ballroom competitions. This international competition was renamed the United States Ballroom Championships/DanceSport. For some time, sponsors and competitors had hoped that ballroom dancing would become a summer sport at the Olympics.

At the airport, Lewis pointed out various European champions arriving, lugging their costumes in specially-made carry-alls.

"Let's find the hotel shuttle," he said as he shepherded the six of us to a line waiting under the sign, "Fountainbleu." Soon, the mini-bus parked in the circular drive in front of the hotel's impressive façade. Inside, we were welcomed by floors and columns of marble and boutiques displaying enticing apparel, jewelry, and high-end tourist gewgaws.

Dance competitors merged with temporary residents. Long lines snaked from the reception desks, where crisply uniformed clerks serviced the patient and the impatient. My senior roommate, Hana, and I were among the disgruntled when we discovered our room was to be in the Smoking Allowed section. We hustled to another line to be relocated. Our needs met, we began the trek to our room. "Why is it dancers are always located farthest from the ballroom?" I asked.

"Well, at least we have a view of the park," she said, pointing to the panorama sixteen floors below.

"That's no park," I said. "That's the Beverly Hills of Miami. See, each mansion has its own dock and yacht."

Hana, a retired nurse, petite, full of joi de vivre, interrupted my perusal of the scene below. "Hadn't we better pick up our programs and let the competition registrar know that we've arrived?"

After hanging our costumes in a spacious closet, we set off down the hallway to the elevator. Once on the main floor and outside the entrance to the ballroom, we saw tables with people checking pre-registrations and selling tickets to evening performances.

"Here's your goody bag," one smiling middle-age woman said as she drew a single line through my name. Inside, I found the thick program for the four days, a T-shirt commemorating the event, various cosmetics, perfume samples, and discount tickets for hotel items.

I accepted the goody bag, thinking, *Not bad for three-thousand dollars.*

Tucking her arm in mine, Hana said, "Let's go back to our room to map out tomorrow's schedule. I don't see Lewis anywhere down here, do you?"

And we reversed the trek.

Seated at the round table abutting the bay-type window, we eagerly flipped the glossy sheets of the two hundred-sixteen page program. Photos of the twenty-four international judges from Norway, Great Britain, Germany, Italy, Canada, South Africa, Slovenia, Russia, Denmark the Netherlands, Austria, Australia, and the United States occupied the first seven pages.

"Hana," I squealed, "here you are on page fourteen! There's your name big as life. Uh oh."

"What?

"The Latin and Rhythm heats are scheduled for tomorrow. I'm used to dancing the Smooths first, in my peach dress wearing my lucky earrings—my comfort zone. I'm more nervous performing the sexy Latins."

Hana didn't comment but suddenly pointed. "Here you are on page twenty."

What a thrill! There I was, Dr. Thea Clark with Lewis Suarez representing the South Bay Dance Club, California.

"I didn't know you were a doctor," she said.

I shrugged. "That's Lewis's little joke. Once he heard about my PhD., he listed it in every program of every comp or show I entered."

"Hey. Time for us to dress for dinner."

No! Your Other Left Foot

A short time later, floating in formals, we joined our group at the traditional first night's banquet. Men in white ties and tails accompanied women of all ages, professionally coiffed with expensive makeup, chatting, strolling, reuniting with friends from other competitions.

I'd attended many a similar banquet, but never on such a grand scale.

"Thea and Hana," Lewis said, "some of us are going to the nightclub below for a while. After you change into something more casual, do you want to join us?"

We two senior citizens nodded in tandem.

Around midnight, dressed in less formal gowns but still in our dance shoes, Hana and I stood outside a black mirrored door from where the energetic beat of a samba leaked. Inside, I found glamour and glitz gyrating happily. *I've died and gone to dancing heaven.*

The next day, my first heat was the cha cha, my nemesis.

Lewis said, "You're good at this now. Just have fun out there. You know that judges give the edge to the woman who looks to be enjoying herself."

He was right, of course, and since I was up against eight other women from all parts of the United States and Canada, I did my best to smile and shine.

Later, at the awards, I was given a First in cha cha, an auspicious beginning for me. In the other Latin dances and swing I did well, earning Firsts and Seconds. Never verbally effusive, Lewis substituted congratulatory bear hugs.

"Tomorrow you'll need to bring your Argentine tango costume with you. You'll have very little time to change after the samba."

We sat at our reserved table with other dancers watching Patty perform a solo at Silver level rumba. Temporarily, I phased out, my mind recalling the week before when Lewis told me I'd overpaid. "How much?" I asked.

"Seventy-five dollars."

"Do they refund that?"

"No, sorry. But that'll cover the fee for another heat."

"What heat?"

"A tango, a Beginners Argentine Tango. Well, actually, it's not graded yet. First time offered at a comp."

"Lewis, you know how I love that dance." The hair on my arms rose and I tingled in expectation.

"We'd do only the first five basic steps," he said.

Already seeing myself dancing, I asked "What about a costume?"

"I suggest a simple straight black short skirt and some sort of fancy top, maybe of lace with sequins or crystals, something to attract attention."

He knew I was hooked.

The Argentine tango and I were simpatico. The music's seductive beat, the complexity of the steps, the war of the sexes, all appealed to me. This dance conversation was like no other.

No! Your Other Left Foot

To the Latino, tango is a state of being, the non-verbal expression of a battle of wills. It is called a man's dance because he determines the choice and order of the complex steps according to how he feels about the music.

The female exerts her choices by accepting the invitation or not, perhaps wanting a better offer. She challenges the male to keep her interested in following him. At first, the moves may appear subdued when you notice how still the upper part of the torso remains. The man's and woman's heads are bent, foreheads touching. When you lower your gaze you see the slightly bent knees and the forward thrust of the two bodies with feet circling and legs intersecting rapidly.

The idea of performing even a simple version of this tango scared the hell out of me.

56

Side Slits

THE STRAIGHT BLACK SATIN SKIRT I'd brought with me had a slit up one side seam. Lewis had opened it up to my hip so I could take long and wide steps. Along this side seam, he sewed a three inch black fringe, then continued it around the hem. Boy, did that fringe flap, swing, and jiggle when I did ochos and ganchos. My black lace, long-sleeved leotard served as a top and an undergarment. I encircled my waist with a wide black leather belt covered with silver and gold studs. New black satin dance shoes waited among fresh tissue for their debut in Miami.

That night, before we strode to the center of the floor to dance a samba among seven other competitors, Lewis asked. "Do you have the tango costume with you?"

I nodded and pointed to my dance bag sitting on the table.

"You won't have time to go to the women's dressing room," he said. "A while ago I talked with John DePalma and he agreed to call a general dance after the samba. That will give you five minutes to change backstage."

"Backstage?"

"Apparently this tango is still new to competitions. No one else has entered this heat."

It took me seconds to register what he was saying. "We are the only ones entered?"

"Yep. How 'bout that?"

"I'll be competing against myself?"

"And you'll be the best one on the floor."

Wearing my blue Latin costume, I danced the samba. As soon as the music stopped, I dashed for my dance bag, then headed for the stairs that led backstage. The usual heavy velvet curtain pulled across the stage separated the judges at their long table from the empty stage. On the other side of the curtain I paused to check my surroundings: one folding metal chair and the usual portable rack on which to hang one's garment bag. No mirror. Muffled laughter and bits of conversation leaked through thin spots in the curtain.

Please God, no one decides to open the curtain while I'm stripped naked. I'd shaken off my crystal studded shoes but kept on the fishnets. I threw the Latin costume over a hanger and pulled on the black lace leotard. Stepping into the black skirt, I zipped up the side. The black satin shoes came next, and lastly, I snapped together the heavy belt.

I stood still, checking myself the best I could without a mirror. A high energy East Coast swing played vigorously for general dancing. Then, setting up the next event, the rain-downpour sound of people clapping and the swishing of people returning to their seats.

That's me. Oh, God! I'm on.

57

Trust Me, He Said

MY TALL, DARK AND HANDSOME partner stood at the bottom of the steps. His black eyes glowed, his smile exuded confidence. Graciously, he extended his hand in invitation. I responded by stretching my neck, lifting my head, expanding my chest and beaming as though I'd won the lottery.

The vast dance floor awaited us. I needed no spotlight to know I was the star. If he hadn't had a tight hold on my hand, I might have fainted. The walk to the center seemed endless.

"Good. Keep that frame. Promenade. Turn, smile at the judges, turn, bow to the audience. Remember, the audience is on your side. They want you to do well. The judges do, too. Trust me."

All eyes focused on us, a spotlight of a different kind.

Lewis turned me to face him. He nodded to the music coordinator. I heard the tango beat of "El Choclo." Lewis raised his left arm. I placed my hand in his. Then, with a deliberate movement, I wrapped my left arm around his shoulder and lightly slid my hand across his back, progressing slowly upwards to his tan neck. Gently, I rested my hand there. I tensed my body. Our foreheads touched.

"Breathe," he whispered.

I felt his warm breath on my cheek as his body moved me backward into a cruzada, then another and still another, and we flowed into the Argentine tango. Everything inside of me shouted, "Go for it. Now!"

The wildness of joy, the exuberant energy, the synchronized movements, all contributed to my search for the out-of-body experience.

Lewis had said: "Trust me. Don't anticipate my moves. Stay in the moment."

My heart sang, my feet slid forward and backward in ochos, cruzadas, sacadas, and molinetes. I added my own embellishments, toe taps and rondos. The floor was my launching pad, I flew within Lewis's arms. Aware only of the music and his hands, body and feet, I flowed in an alpha state of suspended bliss.

Abruptly, he stopped moving. I stood still, immobile in his arms. The music disappeared into the ether. Not a sound anywhere. Silence spread over the ballroom like London fog. "Bow," Lewis said, and he let go of one of my hands so I could move alongside him.

Of course we got a First. There were no other competitors. Yet that First meant more to me than all the others I'd ever earned. A performance of only one hundred and twenty seconds, but what priceless seconds!

Lewis squeezed my hand repeatedly as we exited the floor. I knew he was pleased. He encircled me with his arms, picked me up and swung me around. Setting me down gently, he said, "We did it. Yes. We really did it!"

I knew this moment was important to him. He risked his

reputation trusting me. What if I froze, as I did with Michael during the cha cha at my first competition in Vegas? What if I pulled another Fullerton? But I hadn't. I had found my groove; I was in the zone.

Returning to his teacher persona, Lewis said, "I want you to remember what you did out there today. I want you to always dance that way. Always. You focused on me and it paid off. Today, our dance "conversation" was perfectly synchronized and responsive. How did it feel?"

"I have no words." I hugged myself.

I'd read that the soul of the tango is a blend—the flow of creativity that comes from the freedom to improvise, the agility and precision, the almost operatic intensity of the best tango music. Feeling, more than mastery, makes an Argentine tango dancer. For two minutes, I was a tango dancer.

I continued to take lessons, coachings, and to perform in studio showcases, but the high point of my dancing life remained that perfect moment when I trusted Lewis completely and had faith in myself. Thanks to the mentoring and patience of two wonderful teachers and my own courage, I had changed from a couch potato to someone who, through dancing, had discovered an opening of the spirit.

I am still cha cha-ing along that Yellow Brick Road; now I have a lap top, a clutch of anecdotes, and a life full of Over the Rainbow memories

Acknowledgments

What if:

I'd never met Lewis Suarez or he hadn't suggested I write a book?

Maralys Wills hadn't invited me to join her novel writing class in Yorba Linda?

Walt Golden hadn't suggested we carpool and exchange critiques?

Janet Beech hadn't originated a weekly critique session in Claremont?

My son and daughter-in-law hadn't invited me to stay with them in Upland, offering unconditional encouragement?

Dr. Oda Halverson hadn't healed my wounds from three falls?

Ruth Pitman, Edna Ward, and the staff at Harbor Terrace hadn't patiently listened to my reading of the first half of my book?

I'd never had a chance to be Cinderella going to her own ball?

I'd never risked broken bones, looking foolish, risking bankruptcy?

And finally, what if Allene Symons of Forked Road Press hadn't taken on my memoir as a publishable project?

www.ingramcontent.com/pod-product-compliance
Lightning Source LLC
Chambersburg PA
CBHW031234290426
44109CB00012B/290